Bloom's BioCritiques

Dante Alighieri
Maya Angelou
Jane Austen
James Baldwin
William Blake
Jorge Luis Borges
The Brontë Sisters
Lord Byron
Geoffrey Chaucer
Anton Chekhov
Joseph Conrad
Stephen Crane
Charles Dickens
Emily Dickinson
William Faulkner
F. Scott Fitzgerald
Robert Frost
Ernest Hemingway
Langston Hughes
Zora Neale Hurston
Franz Kafka
Stephen King
Gabriel García Márquez
Herman Melville
Arthur Miller
John Milton
Toni Morrison
Edgar Allan Poe
J.D. Salinger
William Shakespeare
John Steinbeck
Henry David Thoreau
Mark Twain
Alice Walker
Eudora Welty
Walt Whitman
Tennessee Williams

Bloom's BioCritiques

Herman Melville

Edited and with an introduction by
Harold Bloom
Sterling Professor of the Humanities
Yale University

CHELSEA HOUSE
PUBLISHERS
A Haights Cross Communications ◀ Company ®
Philadelphia

©2006 by Chelsea House Publishers, a subsidiary of
Haights Cross Communications.

A Haights Cross Communications ⌁ Company ®

www.chelseahouse.com

Introduction © 2006 by Harold Bloom.

Printed and bound in the United States of America.

10 9 8 7 6 5 4 3 2 1

Library of Congress Cataloging-in-Publication Data
Herman Melville / [edited by] Harold Bloom.
    p. cm. — (Bloom's biocritiques)
  Includes bibliographical references and index.
  ISBN 0-7910-8573-2
  1. Melville, Herman, 1819-1891—Criticism and interpretation. I. Bloom,
Harold. II. Series.

PS2387.H4 2005
813'.3—dc22

                                                                  2005014807

Contributing editor: Randa Dubnick
Cover design by Keith Trego
Cover: © Bettman/CORBIS
Layout by EJB Publishing Services

"The Author of *Typee*, *Omoo*, &c." by Newton Arvin. From Herman Melville,
pp. 77–119. © 1950 by William Sloane Associates, Inc. Renewed 1978 by the
children of author Newton Arvin. Reprinted by permission of HarperCollins
Publishers.

All links and web addresses were checked and verified to be correct at the time
of publication. Because of the dynamic nature of the web, some addresses and
links may have changed since publication and may no longer be valid.

CONTENTS

USER'S GUIDE

These volumes are designed to introduce the reader to the life and work of the world's literary masters. Each volume begins with Harold Bloom's essay "The Work in the Writer" and a volume-specific introduction also written by Professor Bloom. Following these unique introductions is an engaging biography that discusses the major life events and important literary accomplishments of the author under consideration.

Furthermore, each volume includes an original critique that not only traces the themes, symbols, and ideas apparent in the author's works, but strives to put those works into a cultural and historical perspective. In addition to the original critique is a brief selection of significant critical essays previously published on the author and his or her works followed by a concise and informative chronology of the writer's life. Finally, each volume concludes with a bibliography of the writer's works, a list of additional readings, and an index of important themes and ideas.

HAROLD BLOOM

The Work in the Writer

Literary biography found its masterpiece in James Boswell's *Life of Samuel Johnson*. Boswell, when he treated Johnson's writings, implicitly commented upon Johnson as found in his work, even as in the great critic's life. Modern instances of literary biography, such as Richard Ellmann's lives of W.B. Yeats, James Joyce, and Oscar Wilde, essentially follow in Boswell's pattern.

That the writer somehow is in the work, we need not doubt, though with William Shakespeare, writer-of-writers, we almost always need to rely upon pure surmise. The exquisite rancidities of the Problem Plays or Dark Comedies seem to express an extraordinary estrangement of Shakespeare from himself. When we read or attend *Troilus and Cressida* and *Measure for Measure*, we may be startled by particular speeches of Ulysses in the first play, or of Vincentio in the second. These speeches, of Ulysses upon hierarchy or upon time, or of Duke Vincentio upon death, are too strong either for their contexts or for the characters of their speakers. The same phenomenon occurs with Parolles, the military impostor of *All's Well That Ends Well*. Utterly disgraced, he nevertheless affirms: "Simply the thing I am / Shall make me live."

In Shakespeare, more even than in his peers, Dante and Cervantes, meaning always starts itself again through excess or overflow. The strongest of Shakespeare's creatures—Falstaff, Hamlet, Iago, Lear, Cleopatra—have an exuberance that is fiercer than their plays can contain. If Ben Jonson was at all correct in his complaint that "Shakespeare wanted art," it could have been only in a sense that he may not have intended. Where do the personalities of Falstaff or Hamlet touch a limit? What was it in Shakespeare that made *Hamlet* and the two parts of *Henry IV* into "plays unlimited"? Neither Falstaff nor Hamlet will be stopped: their wit, their beautiful, laughing speech, their intensity of being—all these are virtually infinite.

In what ways do Falstaff and Hamlet manifest the writer in the work? Evidently, we can never know, or know enough to answer with any authority. But what would happen if we reversed the question, and asked: How did the work form the writer, Shakespeare?

Of Shakespeare's inwardness, his biography tells us nothing. And yet, to an astonishing extent, Shakespeare created our inwardness. At the least, we can speculate that Shakespeare so lived his life as to conceal the depths of his nature, particularly as he rather prematurely aged. We do not have Shakespeare on Shakespeare, as any good reader of the Sonnets comes to realize: they do not constitute a key that unlocks his heart. No sequence of sonnets could be less confessional or more powerfully detached from the poet's self.

The German poet and universal genius, Goethe, affords a superb contrast to Shakespeare. Of Goethe's life, we know more than every-thing; I wonder sometimes if we know as much about Napoleon or Freud or any other human being who ever has lived, as we know about Goethe. Everywhere, we can find Goethe in his work, so much so that Goethe seems to crowd the writing out, just as Byron and Oscar Wilde seem to usurp their own literary accomplishments. Goethe, cunning beyond measure, nevertheless invested a rival exuberance in his greatest works that could match his personal charisma. The sublime out-rageousness of the Second Part of *Faust*, or of the greater lyric and meditative poems, forms a Counter-Sublime to Goethe's own daemonic intensity.

Goethe was fascinated by the daemonic in himself; we can doubt that Shakespeare had any such interests. Evidently, Shakespeare abandoned his acting career just before he composed *Measure for Measure* and *Othello*. I surmise that the egregious interventions by Vincentio and Iago displace the actor's energies into a new kind of mischief-making, a fresh opening to a subtler playwriting-within-the-play.

But what had opened Shakespeare to this new awareness? The answer is the work in the writer, *Hamlet* in Shakespeare. One can go further: it was not so much the play, *Hamlet*, as the character Hamlet, who changed Shakespeare's art forever.

Hamlet's personality is so large and varied that it rivals Goethe's own. Ironically Goethe's Faust, his Hamlet, has no personality at all, and is as colorless as Shakespeare himself seems to have chosen to be. Yet nothing could be more colorful than the Second Part of *Faust*, which is peopled by an astonishing array of monsters, grotesque devils and classical ghosts.

A contrast between Shakespeare and Goethe demonstrates that in each—but in very different ways—we can better find the work in the person, than we can discover that banal entity, the person in the work. Goethe to many of his contemporaries seemed to be a mortal god. Shakespeare, so far as we know, seemed an affable, rather ordinary fellow, who aged early and became somewhat withdrawn. Yet Faust, though Mephistopheles battles for his soul, is hardly worth the trouble unless you take him as an idea and not as a person. Hamlet is nearly every-idea-in-one, but he is precisely a personality and a person.

Would Hamlet be so astonishingly persuasive if his father's ghost did not haunt him? Falstaff is more alive than Prince Hal, who says that the devil haunts him in the shape of an old fat man. Three years before composing the final *Hamlet*, Shakespeare invented Falstaff, who then never ceased to haunt his creator. Falstaff and Hamlet may be said to best represent the work in the writer, because their influence upon Shakespeare was prodigious. W.H. Auden accurately observed that Falstaff possesses infinite energy: never tired, never bored, and absolutely both witty and happy until Hal's rejection destroys him. Hamlet too has infinite energy, but in him it is more curse than blessing.

Falstaff and Hamlet can be said to occupy the roles in Shakespeare's invented world that Sancho Panza and Don Quixote possess in Cervantes's. Shakespeare's plays from 1610 on (starting with *Twelfth Night*) are thus analogous to the Second Part of Cervantes's epic novel. Sancho and the Don overtly jostle Cervantes for authorship in the Second Part, even as Cervantes battles against the impostor who has pirated a continuation of his work. As a dramatist, Shakespeare manifests the work in the writer more indirectly. Falstaff's prose genius is revived in the scapegoating of Malvolio by Maria and Sir Toby Belch, while Falstaff's darker insights are developed by Feste's melancholic wit. Hamlet's intellectual resourcefulness, already deadly, becomes poisonous in Iago and in Edmund. Yet we have not crossed into the deeper abysses of the work in the writer in later Shakespeare.

No fictive character, before or since, is Falstaff's equal in self-trust. Sir John, whose delight in himself is contagious, has total confidence both in his self-awareness and in the resources of his language. Hamlet, whose self is as strong, and whose language is as copious, nevertheless distrusts both the self and language. Later Shakespeare is, as it were, much under the influence both of Falstaff and of Hamlet, but they tug him in opposite directions. Shakespeare's own copiousness of language is well-nigh incredible: a vocabulary in excess of twenty-one thousand words, almost eighteen hundred of which he coined himself. And of his word-hoard, nearly half are used only once each, as though the perfect setting for each had been found, and need not be repeated. Love for language and faith in language are Falstaffian attributes. Hamlet will darken both that love and that faith in Shakespeare, and perhaps the Sonnets can best be read as Falstaff and Hamlet counterpointing against one another.

Can we surmise how aware Shakespeare was of Falstaff and Hamlet, once they had played themselves into existence? *Henry IV, Part I* appeared in six quarto editions during Shakespeare's lifetime; *Hamlet* possibly had four. Falstaff and Hamlet were played again and again at the Globe, but Shakespeare knew also that they were being read, and he must have had contact with some of those readers. What would it have been like to discuss Falstaff or Hamlet with one of their early readers (presumably also part of their audience at the Globe), if you were the creator of such demiurges? The question would seem nonsensical to most Shakespeare scholars, but then these days they tend to be either ideologues or moldy figs. How can we recover the uncanniness of Falstaff and of Hamlet, when they now have become so familiar?

A writer's influence upon himself is an unexplored problem in criticism, but such an influence is never free from anxieties. The biocritical problem (which this series attempts to explore) can be divided into two areas, difficult to disengage fully. Accomplished works affect the author's life, and also affect her subsequent writings. It is simpler for me to surmise the effect of *Mrs. Dalloway* and *To the Lighthouse* upon Woolf's late *Between the Acts*, than it is to relate Clarissa Dalloway's suicide and Lily Briscoe's capable endurance in art to the tragic death and complex life of Virginia Woolf.

There are writers whose lives were so vivid that they seem sometimes to obscure the literary achievement: Byron, Wilde, Malraux, Hemingway. But most major Western writers do not live that exuberantly, and the greatest of all, Shakespeare, sometimes appears to have adopted the personal mask of colorlessness. And yet there are heroes of literature who struggled titanically with their own eras—Tolstoy, Milton, Victor Hugo—who nevertheless matter more for their works than their lives.

There are great figures—Emily Dickinson, Wallace Stevens, Willa Cather—who seem to have had so little of the full intensity of life when compared to the vitality of their work, that we might almost speak of the work in the work, rather than even of the work in a person. Emily Brontë might well be the extreme instance of such a visionary, surpassing William Blake in that one regard.

I conclude this general introduction to a series of literary bio-critiques by stating a tentative formula or principle for gauging the many ways in which the work influences the person and her subsequent, later work. Our influence upon ourselves is always related to the Shakespearean invention of self-overhearing, which I have written about in several other contexts. Life, as well as poetry and prose, is overheard rather than simply heard. The writer listens to herself as though she were somebody else, and the will to change begins to operate. The forces that live in us include the prior work we have done, and the dreams and waking visions that evade our dismissals.

HAROLD BLOOM

Introduction

There are three nineteenth century prime candidates for the American epic: *Moby-Dick*, *Song of Myself*, and *Adventures of Huckleberry Finn*. If the twentieth century adds a fourth candidate, it might be Thomas Pynchon's *Mason & Dixon* or Cormac McCarthy's *Blood Meridian*, unless one puts together Faulkner's complex saga by excerpting from a number of works, as Malcolm Cowley did in his *Portable Faulkner*. Given a vote, I would select *Moby-Dick*, though the total Walt Whitman seems to me our national writer, with Ralph Waldo Emerson the only possible rival.

Melville the novelist is hardly a one-book man: *Pierre*, though a failure, is a sublime one, and *The Confidence-Man* and *Billy Budd* are remarkable in very different ways. Since Melville at his best was a strong poet, and his *Piazza Tales* are marvelous, the overall achievement fascinates. Nevertheless *Moby-Dick* is unique within the Melville canon, and still a permanent splendor both in American and world literature.

This influence of Shakespeare and of Cervantes is marked and overt in *Moby-Dick*, but the presence of Melville's major precursors does not limit the majesty or the originality. I once found myself affirming that Ahab both was and was *not* a hero-villain on two consecutive pages of a book I had written. My self-contradiction carried me back to childhood, when I identified with the *Pequod's* obsessed captain, and forward to old age, when I shudder at the consequences of Ahab's quest. Like Macbeth, Ahab provokes our ambivalences.

But I do not think that Melville is equivocal about Ahab. How can a writer (unless he is Shakespeare) distance himself from a protagonist as urgent as Ahab?

> If man will strike, strike through the mask! How can the prisoner reach outside except by thrusting through the wall? To me, the white whale is that wall, shoved near me. Sometimes I think there's naught beyond. But 'tis enough. He tasks me; he heaps me; I see in him outrageous strength, with an inscrutable malice sinewing it. That inscrutable thing is chiefly what I hate; and be the white whale agent, or be the white whale principal, I will wreak that hate upon him. Talk not to me of blasphemy, man; I'd strike the sun if it insulted me.

How different are the two uses of "strike"! To strike through the mask is to defy one's own nihilism, but to strike the sun is to refuse acknowledgement that we are here to be insulted. Melville's *Pequod* is Quaker-owned, but Starbuck is the only Quaker, indeed the only Christian, on board. Ahab has gone from Quakerism to pure Zoroastrianism and ends as a Promethean Gnostic. Ishmael, the narrator, is an Emersonian Platonist, and the rest of the crew are animists, Zoroastrian dualists, atheists, or sublime idol-worshippers like Queequeg.

Ishmael is one of the most problematic narrators in all of literature. We are told that "Ahab's Ahab," a firm identity, but Ishmael is and is not Melville, is and is not Ahab, and Starbuck wonders whether Ahab is Ahab. Confronted by Moby-Dick, at once Leviathan and Behemoth, do we not all become Job? Under Melville's influence, Ralph Ellison's Invisible Man will fuse Jonah and Job, but the fusion exists already in Ishmael/Melville

Ahab's father, he says, is the Demiurge, the false creator-god (or botcher) of this cosmos, but Ahab favors his mother, the abyss, which preceded our cosmological emptiness. Ishmael, a wonder-wounded auditor of Ahab, despite his sense of Ahab's greatness, seems closer to Emerson's Platonism than to Ahab's Gnosticism. The immense beauty of Melville's novel comes to us through Ishmael, who perhaps represents the poet in Melville more than the novelist. Ishmael has a real touch of Shakespearean detachment in him, but Ahab is about as detached as King Lear was.

Huck Finn and "Walt Whitman" move us to poignant affection, while Ahab seems beyond our capacity to absorb him. Faulkner's Ahabian heroes are not on Melville's huge scale. Ahab remains still the tragic version of the American hero, epic in scope, doom-eager always.

NEIL HEIMS

Biography of Herman Melville

He did not build himself in with plans; he wrote right on; and so doing, got deeper and deeper into himself; and like a resolute traveler, plunging through a baffling woods, at last was rewarded for his toils.

—(*Mardi*: Ch. 180)

An Unknown Man

In the spring of 1870, Herman Melville stopped into the Gansevoort Hotel in New York City in lower Manhattan, not far from the docks on which he worked for $4 a day as a customs inspector. At the concession stand in the lobby he "bought a paper of tobacco by way of introducing myself: Then I said to the person who served me: Can you tell me what this word 'Gansevoort' means? Is it the name of a man? And if so, who was this Gansevoort?" Before the person behind the counter could answer, "a solemn gentleman at a remote table spoke up: 'Sir,' said he putting down his newspaper, 'this hotel and the street of the same name are called after a rich family who in old times owned a great deal of property hereabouts.'" This response infuriated Melville.

The dense ignorance of this solemn gentleman,—his knowing nothing of the hero of Fort Stanwix, aroused such an indignation in my breast, that disdaining to enlighten his benighted soul, I left the place without further colloquy. Repairing to the philosophic privacy of the District Office I then moralized upon the instability of human glory and the evanescence of—many other things. (Parker 2002, 703)

Gansevoort, in fact, was Melville's mother's maiden name, and it was the given name of his long-dead and revered older brother as well as his own middle name. It was the name of an old American family of Dutch extraction, which had emigrated to Albany, New York, when New York was still called New Amsterdam and when Albany was still known as Fort Orange. There the Gansevoorts settled, prospered as brewers, and married with the "best" Dutch families. Their pedigree was based not, however, on wealth or social position as much as on the deeds of Herman Melville's grandfather, his mother's father, Peter Gansevoort, whose heroism had earned him a place in history books.

In 1777, Peter Gansevoort and a company of grenadiers defended Fort Stanwix in the Mohawk River Valley from Iroquois troops fighting on the side of England and blocked the British advance to Albany. John Adams, who later became the second president of the United States, commended Gansevoort's valor in a letter to his wife, Abigail. After the war Peter was granted timber lands in Albany, where he set up a saw mill. President Thomas Jefferson "appointed him military agent of the northern department of the United States" in 1802, and in 1809, "President James Madison appointed him brigadier general in the army of the United States." Gilbert Stuart, the American portrait painter, noted particularly for his portraits of George Washington, painted his picture (Parker 1996, 4). Peter Gansevoort died in 1812, but remained a legend in the family. He was always referred to by his descendents as "the hero of Fort Stanwix," and Stanwix became one of the names that descendents in the Gansevoort family regularly bestowed upon their offspring, as Melville did in 1851 on his younger son.

Melville's indignation at the tobacco concession in the Gansevoort Hotel was not only at the pompous ignorance of American revolutionary history and at the ignorance of his own family's celebrated role in that history. His last words signal the real wound, leaving it unsaid and only suggested—when he meditated on evanescence—in the evasive phrase "many other things."

A meditation on the "instability of human glory" would inevitably draw Melville away from the evanescence of his mother's family's glory and to the evaporation of his own. In 1870, for four years already, the author of *Moby-Dick* had vanished from the public eye and spent each of his days as a customs inspector on the docks of New York City poring over freight lists and passenger lists on the decks of newly-arrived ships, checking them against cargo and passengers, preparatory to unloading and disembarkation. He was to continue in this position until 1885, when he retired and maintained the life of quiet authorship he had already been practicing for many years, writing for the sake of writing— almost as a vice, as a solitary, secret pursuit—not for the sake of the market, publishing his work himself in small numbers or leaving it unpublished, as he did the manuscript of his great last work, *Billy Budd*.

As a literary man, Melville was all but a forgotten man. He was disheartened not only by the lack of public recognition but by the public vilification of his work and by the contemptuous regard of many in his own family for his career as an author and for the books he had written. His wife Lizzie's brother Lem wrote to his brother Sam, when, in 1855, Melville was working on *The Confidence Man*, "I believe [Melville] is now preparing another book for the press.... I have no great confidence in the success of his productions" (Robertson-Lorant, 359). A few years earlier Lem had written his parents from London that Melville wrote "books that nobody can read," and that he "wish[ed] very much he could be persuaded to leave off writing for a few years." (Robertson-Lorant, 303) In their contempt, his family was only following what seemed to be a universal judgment. When Melville did attempt to step back into the open as a writer with the publication of short poems in a volume called *Battle Pieces* after the Civil War, his efforts were castigated, his family's disapprobation was validated, a sense of humiliation was his reward, and further withdrawal was his response.

At the time of his encounter with the philistine in the lobby of the Gansevoort Hotel as he was buying tobacco, Melville was beginning a long poem, *Clarel*, which, when it was published in the centennial year of 1876, did nothing to release him from the burden of literary opprobrium but rather confirmed opinion that he was untalented and laboring under a delusion of nearly insane proportion. So little was writing seen as his work, that his wife, Lizzie, writing in 1885 to

Melville's cousin Kate Lansing spoke of Melville's job as a customs inspector as an "occupation" which "is a great thing to him," (Parker 2002, 871) when, in fact, it was wearing him out, keeping him away from his writing desk, and was a daily reminder of what he was not, a successful author, acclaimed for his work, who, by writing, was able to support his family.

That Melville brooded daily, however, on his exile from his proper calling is unlikely. His exercise in stoical acceptance of his lot seems to have been successful, and he was described around 1884 as bearing "nothing of the appearance of a man disappointed in life, but rather had an air of perfect contentment, and his conversation had much of his jovial, let-the-world-go-as-it-will spirit" (Parker 2002, 872). But it may have taken a good deal of time and aging to achieve this equanimity, for in 1859, he appeared to a visitor to have the "air ... of one who has been soured by opposition and criticism.... his attitude seemed ... that of a man whose hand is against every man's and every man's against him" (Parker 2002, 399).

At home, among his family, too, it is not clear that he was always an adept practitioner of contented resignation. Although there is no specific documentation or proof of the actual circumstances or events, there are suggestions in family correspondence and lingering rumors that Melville was a man with a temper which could explode into violent acts and a tongue and a temperament which could demean, and that his domestic situation periodically became strained. In 1855, Lizzie's cousin Samuel Hay Savage wrote, "Lizzy no doubt alone has had many of life's real trials to conflict with.... Herman I hope has had no more of the ugly attacks" (Robertson-Lorant, 371f.). Whether the "ugly attacks" refers to the bouts of physical pain and sciatica which plagued him or to outbursts of violence is not clear. Around 1867 Lizzie seems to have expressed a wish to separate. "The whole family understands the case," Lizzie's brother Sam wrote in a kind of family white paper, "and the thing has resolved itself into the mere question of my sister's willingness to say the word.... I do not think it could be managed better than by having her at our house and by keeping her there and carefully preventing her husband from seeing her" (Parker 2002, 629ff).

In the later part of his lifetime, Herman Melville's name, although disesteemed in literary circles, however, was not unknown. He was remembered for his first two books and for failing to meet the promise they announced—or so it seemed to those who judged literary careers—

primarily by abandoning the sort of work and workmanship those books represented and by attempting things more complex and less accessible. The first two books, *Typee* and *Omoo* were great triumphs for Melville. They had made him not only a celebrity, but had endowed him with a threatening sexual mystique because of their exotic locations and because of their pagan, as well as sometimes erotic, subject matter. Some of the critical responses to them, however, were harbingers of future difficulties.

AN AUSPICIOUS BEGINNING AND ITS VICISSITUDES: TYPEE AND OMOO

In 1839, twenty-year-old Herman Melville signed on to the *St. Lawrence*, a passenger and cargo ship as a hand, and sailed to Liverpool, England, beginning a series of nautical adventures which lasted until 1844, when he returned to his mother's house in Lansigburgh, New York, and began writing about his voyages and the places he had seen, particularly the South Sea islands of Polynesia. Writing seems to have grown naturally both out of his adventures and out of his sailor's life. During his years at sea, he was in the habit of sitting on deck with mates at night under a vast sky. Surrounded by the endless ocean, he spun yarns about his adventures to amuse his shipmates and to while away the time.

Typee, his first book, published in 1846, was presented to the public not as a novel but as a true account of his travel adventures. In fact, the Harper brothers, the first American publisher Melville submitted the book to, rejected *Typee* because, they asserted, "it was impossible that it could be true and therefore was without real value" (Parker 1996, 376). Their objection reveals a streak of Puritanism, which, as one of its principles, subordinated the luxuriance of fiction to the plain truth of fact, and it was Puritanism which would soon begin to undermine Melville's career even after *Typee* found a British and an American publisher. In actuality, *Typee was* a true account *shaped* into a fiction, embellished by authorial re-creation, as first novels often are. Indeed, all Melville's fiction is to some degree autobiographical, whether reconstructing and reconfiguring concrete, psychological, or spiritual events of his life. Because, however, the spirit of the time regarded a "true" account to be of higher worth than a fiction and literalism a more accurate rendition of truth than imagination, Melville was at pains repeatedly (although it seems in retrospect somewhat disingenuously) to guarantee that *Typee* and *Omoo* were true accounts of actual events and not imaginative creations. In *Typee*, Melville tells the story of his voyage as a crewman on the *Acushnet* (called the *Dolly*), his desertion because of the oppressive discipline of the ship's tyrannical captain, his adventures on a strange, paradisiacal but cannibal island, and his escape from the island. In the Puritan but also democratically egalitarian climate of early mid-eighteenth-century America, as well as in Victorian England, where prudery at home was combined with curiosity about "primitive" cultures abroad, the story of a tropical people who were socially cooperative, sexually liberal, and on occasion, cannibalistic was particularly fascinating.

But the elements of the book and the conditions of the culture in which the book appeared, which made *Typee* fascinating, also made it censurable. *Typee* was published first in England by John Murray (who, like the Harper brothers, was troubled by the feeling that the book was a novel rather than a solid account of the author's actual experience—but Murray was not deterred from publishing it). After its British publication *Typee* was published in the United States by the firm of Wylie & Putnam. Initially, British reviews of *Typee* were good. It was called "a book ... full of fresh and richly-coloured matter," and it was valued as an eye-witness account "by a person who has lived with [the natives of the Polynesian Islands] in their own fashion, and as near as may be upon terms of social equality." Melville's depiction of Polynesian life was hailed as "incomparably the most vivid and forcible that has ever been laid before the public" (Parker 1996, 400). Soon, however, the nature of what Melville was depicting became an issue for reviewers and a matter of contention.

"One or two voluptuous scenes might well have been expunged, and the high strain of admiration for savage life and uncivilized customs somewhat moderated," one British reviewer complained. Another objected that "seldom have savages found so zealous a vindicator of their morals; rarely, too has Christianity owned so ungrateful a son." In this matter of the conflict of cultures, Melville suffered further criticism regarding his treatment of Christian missionaries, whose efforts at converting Pagans to Christianity he found misguided and even cruel: "it is remarkable," the reviewer in the British journal *Critic* wrote, "that [Melville] never speaks of [missionaries] but in terms of downright disrespect, of ridicule as often as he can, or to charge them with gross and willful exaggeration in their statements, or with credulity or blindness in their dealings with the natives," who were, after all, "idol worshippers."

Melville, in conclusion, was condemned for not having "the real interests of Christianity very seriously at heart" (Parker 1996, 401–2).

Publication of the novel in the United States brought the same popular success which *Typee* enjoyed throughout the British Empire, as well as focus on the same aspects: the pleasures of a primitive culture with a relaxed sexual ethos and concern about Melville's regard (or *dis*regard) for Christian civilization. Melville's attitude towards Christian missionaries soon came under particular scrutiny. Evert Duyckinck, writing on March 21, 1846, in the New York *Morning News* supported Melville's representation of "missionary rule in the Sandwich Islands as for the most part a vulgar and miserable misgovernment," and he pointed out furthermore that Melville is balanced in his criticism because he realized that "we are not to charge all the evils arising ... in those islands exclusively upon the missionaries." The major focus of this review and of others, too however, was literary, noting that *Typee* "is lightly but vigorously written," and "no work ... gives a freer and more effective picture of barbarian life" (Parker 1996, 410–11).

But the April issue of the New York *American Review* signaled a sea change for Melville's literary career which would have profound and lasting consequences. The writer objected that "remarks concerning the Missionaries of the Sandwich Islands ... we think are prejudiced and unfounded" (Parker 1996, 415). That was the opening salvo, but the real attack came in a review in the New York *Evangelist*, "the principal organ of the Presbyterian church," on April 9, 1846. "The work was made," the reviewer contended,

> not for America, but for a circle, and that not the highest, in London, where theatres, opera-dancers, and voluptuous prints have made such unblushing walks along the edge of modesty.... We are sorry that such a volume should have been allowed a place in the 'Library of American Books'.... [T]he work in hand ... while everybody will admit it is written with an attractive vivacity, and (except where it palpably lies) with great good humor ... cannot escape severe condemnation (Parker 1996, 416).

And it did not. Attack followed attack on two heads: one, regarding doubt as to the authenticity of the narrative and the second, faulting the moral character of the author for his criticism of Christian missionaries, his "panegyric on cannibal delights," and his "apostrophe to the spirit of savage felicity." His book was not just getting a bad review. Melville himself was being called a "traducer ... who condemn[ed] ... the ripening fruit of the gospel of Christ" (Parker 1996, 432). Melville was distressed. What had seemed like a literary triumph was threatening to become a debacle. And his critics' victory over his book was in fact realized when John Wiley, one of the principals of the house publishing *Typee* in the United States, and a Presbyterian, informed Melville, in April 1846, when a second printing was necessary, that printer's errors of the first edition would be "corrected." But correction was, in fact, a euphemism Wiley used to signify expurgation. The second edition of *Typee*, with offending passages about Christian missionaries and Polynesian sexuality deleted by Wiley in order to bring the book into better conformity with Protestant doctrine, was called a Revised Edition (Parker 1996, 417; 440f.).

Melville was resentful but compliant. He tried to make the best of it by gathering good reviews to append to the front of the book, and he felt vindicated when Richard Tobias Greene, his companion Toby in *Typee*, revealed himself to the Buffalo *Commercial Advertiser*, thereby validating Melville's claims to the book's authenticity. Melville wrote for the revised edition not only a sequel dealing with Toby's reappearance and their meeting, but also a prefatory note saying, "The reception given to *Typee* has induced the author to believe it worthy of revision. And as the interest of the book chiefly consists in its being the history of a remarkable adventure, in revising it, several passages, wholly unconnected with that adventure, have been rejected as irrelevant" (Parker 1996, 446). Melville's niece, Charlotte, born in 1859, in later life reported, nevertheless, that she had heard her aunt, Melville's sister, Kate, say that Melville "was very cut up that in all later editions—all mention of the Missionary's [*sic*] was omitted. He saw how much evil they were doing and thought it should be known" (Parker 1996, 440).

Despite all the ravages perpetrated upon his book and upon himself, Melville was a successful author. Before even seeing it, his British publisher, John Murray, promised him "as liberal an offer" as possible for *Omoo*, his next book, which was to continue the adventures narrated in *Typee*, and which Melville had already begun. Yet even at this early stage of his career, because of the nature of the controversies that surrounded his work, there was, in his fame, an admixture of notoriety, which would increase and become fatal.

Melville's fall from literary significance, however, did not happen all at once. When he offered *Omoo* to Frederick Saunders, an editor at Harpers, saying, "I suppose there is no use of offering this to the house?" Saunders replied, "Mr. Harper is in his carriage now at the door about to start to Europe. I'll go ask him." In response, "jumping into his carriage and driving off," Harper cried, "Take it at once." Harper, a Methodist, not a Presbyterian, had no connection with missionaries and had regretted the unsound business decision of having rejected *Typee* (Parker 1996, 470).

MARRIAGE

In 1846, Melville proposed to Elizabeth Shaw, the daughter of Lemuel Shaw, a pillar of Boston Society and the chief justice of the Supreme Court of Massachusetts from 1830 until his death in 1860. Lemuel Shaw was also an old friend of the Melville family, who had once been engaged to marry Melville's aunt, his father's sister, Nancy Wroe Melville. She died in 1813, however, but remained a treasured memory for Shaw, who carried two pictures of her and a love letter from her in his wallet all his life (Parker 1996, 11; 300). Shaw also had particular affection for Melville's father, Allan Melvill—the final "e" was a later addition to the name—and it was very likely Shaw who composed the notice of Allan Melvill's death, which appeared in the Boston *Daily Advertiser and Patriot* on February 3, 1832 (Parker 1996, 62). In 1834, Judge Shaw wrote Allan's widow, Melville's mother, Maria, that he felt "deep interest & solicitude" for her children, who were also the children of one of his "oldest & best friends," and promised, "I shall at all times & under all circumstances, do all in my power, to promote their best interests." He was true to his word (Parker 2002, 307f.). Even when the rest of his family had lost faith in Melville as a writer and as a reasonably sound man, Lemuel Shaw did not, aiding him financially as well as supporting him by believing in him.

Melville had known Elizabeth Shaw from childhood when his family had visited the Shaws. After his brother Gansevoort had seen Melville off from New Bedford when he set out on his sea adventures in December 1840, Gansevoort, newly a lawyer, traveled to Boston to visit Judge Shaw to ask him for help, especially to see if he could pay for a sea voyage for Gansevoort himself, to the Caribbean, for the sake of his health, which was poor, poorer in fact than he knew, for he would die not many years later, in 1846, in London. Judge Shaw gave him $150. In September 1841, Gansevoort accompanied his (and Melville's) sister, Helen, from the Melville home in Lansingburgh, New York, to Lennox, Massachusetts, where Shaw had brought his family, that they might be with him as he conducted the business of the state court which was scheduled to convene there.

It was then that Helen Melville met Elizabeth Shaw and the two became close friends. Helen wrote to her sister Augusta, "Mrs. Shaw insists upon my making her a long visit this winter in Boston; both herself and her husband gave me the most pressing & earnest invitation, & Mama says I may go" (Parker 1996, 301). Helen spent several extended periods with the Shaws in Boston. In February 1842, she met Charles Dickens there, and Elizabeth visited Helen in Lansingburgh, too.

Documentary evidence is lacking which might indicate what Melville did after he docked in Boston in October 1844, returning from his nearly four years at sea. But it seems likely that he visited his Boston relatives. Learning from them of his sister's intimacy with Elizabeth Shaw and recalling the judge, his father's close friend, it is probable that he then went to visit the Shaws. There he formed the sort of bond with Judge Shaw which would allow him to dedicate *Typee* to him "affectionately" and "gratefully" two years later and the kind of closeness with Elizabeth which would allow him to propose marriage to her (Parker 1996, 301; 305).

Omoo was published in 1847, the same year Melville and Elizabeth Shaw, called Lizzie, were married. Although he had become famous, Melville had not become rich from his writing, nor even was he in a position to support a wife on his earnings. Therefore, before their marriage took place, Melville traveled to Washington, D.C. hoping to procure a government job in the Treasury Department. He had connections, Senator John A. Dix, a friend of his uncle, Peter Gansevoort, and William L. Marcy, the Secretary of War and formerly the governor of New York, whom Melville's brother Gansevoort had supported for that office in 1844. But Melville himself had done the party no service, and received no patronage. He returned to Boston, nevertheless with confidence in the success he believed *Omoo* would bring him, but Judge Shaw, despite his fondness for Melville and despite seeing his daughter's love for Melville, did not agree at once to their becoming engaged (Robertson-Lorant, 155).

When he returned from Washington, Melville first stayed in New York City, but soon returned to his mother's house in Lansigburgh to finish *Omoo*. He found himself, however, repeatedly distracted by thoughts of Lizzie and marriage, and he traveled several times to Boston to be with her. Melville's mother, Maria, wrote about the situation to her daughter Augusta who was visiting the Shaws urging her to press for the marriage: "I can see no reason why it should be postponed any longer." She suggested that Lizzie set the date and that Herman and Lizzie live in the house in Lansingburgh with her. In that way Herman would be able to support Lizzie. She wrote that they ought not "wait for an uncertain future, which none of us can penetrate" and that if Lizzie didn't set a date, Herman would not "be able to attend to his book." The couple agreed to live in Lansingburgh and Judge Shaw capitulated, ensuring his daughter's future by establishing a trust fund providing her with a yearly income. In addition, Judge Shaw actually did give Melville two thousand dollars to rent a house in New York City, and the newlyweds, when they returned from their honeymoon, lived less than a month with Melville's mother in Lansingburgh (Parker 1996, 522f.).

In order to avoid the kind of gawking that the author of *Typee* would attract, the wedding was a private ceremony in Judge Shaw's house on Beacon Hill in Boston on August 4, 1847 (Robertson-Lorant, 159). For their honeymoon trip, Herman and Lizzie went to the White Mountains of New Hampshire and then on to Montreal, Quebec, by way of Lake Champlain (Parker 1996, 546).

Omoo was published by John Murray in England on March 27, 1847, a month before the Harper Brothers edition came out in the United States. (Publication in England preceded publication in the United States in order to protect Murray's investment from piracy; since no copyright laws applied, any British publisher might have printed an edition from the American edition.) The first printing sold out in a week. Despite the popularity of his books, Melville made very little money from them. During the first two and a half years after publication, *Typee* earned $1,465.49, and for the rest of his life brought Melville no more than $2,000 (Robertson-Lorant, 157). Additionally, Melville ate into his profits because he bought books and charged them to his publisher against future sales, ultimately becoming indebted to the Harpers.

MARDI: FROM REPORTAGE TO ROMANCE

Omoo's popular success was accompanied by the same sort of critical storm which *Typee* encountered. It was praised for "brilliant and captivating style ... warmth ... tropical luxuriance ... genial flow of humor ... happy enthusiasm." In the *Brooklyn Eagle*, Walter Whitman, not yet Walt, described its style as "richly good-natured," and wrote that it was "thorough entertainment—not so light as to be tossed aside for its flippancy, nor so profound as to be tiresome." But in the *American Review*, *Omoo* was called "venomous, and ... venereous," which was tantamount to calling it pornographic. It showed "cool, sneering wit," and a "perfect want of *heart*" (Robertson-Lorant, 156f.).

Important as these condemnations were to the future of Melville's career and to forming *his* attitude about writing in the marketplace, they were, fundamentally, not about literary issues. Judged as literature, *Omoo* was generally considered a weaker book than *Typee*, not its equal. "*Typee* is as pure gold to the lacquer of *Omoo*," was the way the difference between the two books was formulated by the reviewer in the London *Sun* (Parker 1996, 503). The consequence of this alleged difference was manifest in the sales figures John Murray, his London publisher, sent Melville in order to temper Melville's demands when they began to negotiate a contract for his next book.

> Of *Typee* I printed 5000 Copies and have sold 4104. Of *Omoo*, 4000 and have sold 2512—Thus I have gained by the former 51-2.3 [51 pounds, 2 shillings, 3 pence] & by the latter am a loser of 57-16-10 [57 pounds, 16 shillings, 10 pence]. I do not willingly enter into such details but this is bona fide the state of the Case. I should not have entered into such details with an Author but that it is evident from your Manner of Writing that you and your friend[s] suppose me to be reaping immense advantages in which you ought to be participating—understand *I* pray that I do not eventually expect to be a loser but I *cannot anticipate* from what has occurred that I shall be any great gainer except in credit as the publisher of these two Books.

Murray offered to look at *Mardi*, and if it seemed promising, he would advance Melville a hundred guineas. He concluded by stating once again his objection that the books were seen as "fictions," and the public's "feeling of being tricked ... impedes their sales" (Parker 1996, 575f.). Melville responded as if to a dare:

> To be blunt: the work I shall next publish will in downright earnest [be] a "Romance of Polynisian Adventure".... [T]he reiterated imputation of being a romancer in disguise has at last pricked me into a resolution to show those who may take any interest in the matter, that a real romance of mine is no *Typee* or *Omoo*, & is made of different stuff altogether.... I have long thought that Polynisia furnished a great deal of rich poetical material that has never been employed hitherto in works of fancy; and which to bring out suitably, required only that play of freedom & invention accorded only to the Romancer & poet.... [P]roceeding in my narrative of facts I began to feel an invincible distaste for the same; & a longing to plume my pinions for a flight, & felt irked, cramped & fettered by plodding along with dull common places,—So suddenly abandoning the thing alltogether, [*sic*] I went to work heart & soul at a romance.... It is something new I assure you, & original if nothing more.... It opens like a true narrative-like *Omoo* for example, on ship board—& the romance & poetry of the thing thence grow continuously, till it becomes a story wild enough I assure you & with a meaning too. (Parker 1996, 590)

In *Mardi*, Melville abandoned any pretence that he was writing non-fiction. This tale's fancifulness is not the result of the peculiar realities of far-away cultures. *Mardi* is an allegory in hard-wrought prose regarding the nature of existence in the guise of adventures on a whaling expedition in a manner indebted to Rabelais, Sir Thomas Browne, and the Samuel Johnson of *Rasselas*. Melville had indeed begun to be restless intellectually as he had been, earlier, physically, and needed to travel in his thoughts as he had upon the seas. The experience he was drawing upon now was not only the result of travel, but of reading, thought, and reverie. It was, after going to sea, Melville's second step in his work of creating himself.

Melville's need to fashion himself independently lay, perhaps, in his early experience of having been repeatedly overthrown by circumstances for which he bore no responsibility, over which he had no control, but which, nevertheless, formed a life for him which seemed to be dictated by a frustrating and malevolent fate.

MELVILLE'S EARLY LIFE

Herman Melville was born on August 1, 1819, in New York City to Maria Gansevoort Melvill and Allan Melvill, the second of their eight children. Allan Melvill was descended from a family as distinguished as his wife's. Allan's father, Herman Melville's paternal grandfather, Thomas Melvill, was just as celebrated a Revolutionary War figure as Melville's maternal grandfather, Peter Gansevoort. Thomas Melvill, born in Boston in 1751 to a Scottish immigrant, was a graduate of Princeton University. He had intended to become a minister but became a merchant instead. In 1773, he participated in the legendary Boston Tea Party. Along with Samuel Adams and other Boston colonists, who called themselves the Sons of Liberty and believed that "taxation without representation is tyranny," he boarded a ship docked in Boston Harbor and dumped crates of tea into the water. After 1776, Thomas Melvill served in the Continental Army, and after the war, George Washington appointed him Inspector of Customs. The appointment was renewed by Presidents Adams, Jefferson, and Madison. In 1811, Madison appointed him Naval Officer for the District of Boston and Charlestown. These offices were not merely honorary; in them, Thomas Melvill profited richly as a tradesman.

He had two sons, Thomas Jr., the elder, born in 1776, and Allan, Herman Melville's father, born in 1782. Rather than sending them to college, he sent them to Paris. Allan's stay in France not only made him fluent in French but endowed him with a debonair sensibility and an aesthetic refinement, which showed in everything about him—from the way he dressed to the gracefulness of his prose and the polish of his verse to his eye for quality merchandise. This last attribute was important because his sojourn in France was intended not only to be for the cultivation of a gentleman. He was there as his father's agent, acquiring merchandise to export to the United States. As proficient as he was in good taste and as practiced as a connoisseur, so was he deficient in business acumen. From the start of his mercantile career in 1802 until his final bankruptcy in 1830, he made poor business decisions, embarked on foolish ventures, associated with questionable partners, borrowed money unwisely, and spent and lived beyond his means (Parker 1996, 7).

On October 9, 1830, at the age of forty-eight, under cover of darkness, Allan Melvill, accompanied by his eleven-year-old son, Herman, fled New York City. Avoiding arrest by his creditors, and only a step ahead of the police, they sailed on the *Swiftsure*, out of New York Harbor, for the safety of Albany, where his wife Maria and Melville's older brother Gansevoort had gone with their furniture the day before. In Albany, destitute and dependent, the entire family, Allan and Maria Melvill and their eight children, were put up in a house which Maria's brother, Peter Gansevoort, rented for them. They lived on hand-outs from Peter and from Allan's father, old Major Thomas Melvill, the hero of the Boston Tea Party, which had to supplement Allan's small wages as a hired clerk in an Albany cap and fur store (Parker 1996, 50f.).

Until the flight to Albany, for his first eleven years, Herman Melville enjoyed a life of privilege in New York City in a renowned and apparently wealthy family. His parents lived in fine houses, took splendid vacations in other fine houses owned by members of the extended families, had numerous servants, participated in grand social entertainments, and supplied their children with tutors. Allan Melvill, until the crash, was a man of genial spirit, and his wife, until the crash, was a good-natured and loving mother. Melville, she wrote indulgently on December 29, 1824, when he was five, "attends school regularly but does not appear so fond of his Book as to injure his health—He has turned into a great tease, & daily puts Gansevoorts [*sic*] Patience to flight, who cannot bear to be 'plagued by such a little Fellow.'" (Parker 1996, 28) His father's evaluation of him in a letter to Melville's uncle, Peter Gansevoort, prior to Melville's visit with his uncle expands but does not contradict his mother's. Melville is "honest hearted," but also "very backward in speech & somewhat slow in comprehension." Nevertheless, "as far as he understands men & things," he is, his father wrote, "both solid & profound, & of a docile & aimiable [*sic*] disposition" (Parker 1996, 35).

Five and a half years later, when Melville was attending the New-York Male High School, his father wrote of him to his own father, Herman's grandfather, Major Thomas Melvill, that Melville "without being a bright Scholar ... maintains a respectable standing & would proceed further, if he could only be induced to study more." Allan

Melvill concluded that since Melville is "a most amiable & innocent child, I cannot find it in my heart to coerce him, especially as he seems to have chosen Commerce as a favorite pursuit, whose practical activity can well dispense with much book knowledge" (Parker 1996, 48). The future would show Allan Melvill was as mistaken about his son as he was about his own business affairs, for although study and book knowledge were to be indispensable to his son, he would prove nearly as wanting in shrewdness in commercial matters as his father.

In Albany, Melville attended the Albany Academy and was awarded, in August, 1831, the "first best in his class" in "ciphering," i.e., arithmetic. But his academic career was soon interrupted by his father's death, precipitated by a return journey from New York City the second week in December. Allan had gone on business related to his debts in bitter cold weather. On the journey back he traveled sometimes in an open carriage, and he crossed the frozen Hudson to Albany one night on foot. The last weeks before his collapse were frantic with attempts to attend to business. On January 8, 1832, Allan's health gave way completely, both physically and mentally. In his wife Maria's words, he was "depriv'd of his intellect." He died on January 28, 1832 (Parker 1996, 56ff.).

Because of their father's death, Gansevoort and Melville withdrew from school. Gansevoort, sixteen, with the help of his mother's brother, his Uncle Peter, established himself in a fur and cap business (Parker 1996, 676). Twelve-year-old Melville began working in June as a clerk at $150 a year in the New York State Bank in Albany, of which his Uncle Peter was one of the directors. Soon after Melville began to work at the bank, Albany was threatened by a cholera epidemic and Maria Melvill fled the city with her eight children for Pittsfield, Massachusetts, where her brother-in-law, Allan's brother Thomas Melvill Jr., had a farm. As soon as Uncle Peter learned of Maria's flight with the children, he insisted that Melville had no leave from the bank and that he must return to Albany, which he did.

Melville worked in the bank six days a week until 1834, filing, copying, and running errands. Not only was he confined by his job, but during the summer of 1832, he was confined to his house—his Uncle Peter's house—when not at the bank, for going out into the streets during a time of cholera was too dangerous. Uncle Peter had a capacious library, however, and Melville spent his time reading. Nevertheless, his education was neglected by all his relatives, who were wealthy enough to have provided him with one had they cared to, but the burden of the debt his father left at his death rankled them, and even when Lemuel Shaw, as Allan Melvill's trustee, proposed to the family that they each contribute to a fund for the widow and children, his proposal was rejected, causing Maria Melvill to write him, "The apparent utter desertion of the Grandparents & Aunts to my Children, since the Death of their Father, is singular, & to me seems inexplicable" (Parker 1996, 82).

The main support of the family was Gansevoort's fur and cap business. Just when it was going well, in May 1834, and Gansevoort was seeing the possibility of pulling the family out of debt through his hard work, his fur factory, but not his store, burned down, causing him a loss of between $1,500 and $2,000. The loss was severe but not fatal. Gansevoort began again, dismissing his employees and taking Melville from the bank and setting him to work in the store. That was not the only change in Melville's life, for it was about this time that he became a member of the Albany Young Men's Association, a "mutual improvement society" where he joined with other youths to discuss the books they were reading and to practice the arts of public speaking and debate. In the spring of 1835, he enrolled at the Albany Classical School, where, according to his teacher there, Charles West, Melville showed "deftness" at writing "themes or compositions and [was] fond of doing it, while the great majority of the students dreaded the task." While in school Melville developed an interest in teaching and returned to the Albany Academy to study Latin in the fall of 1836 after a five year absence, and studied there until March 1837 (Robertson-Lorant, 60). That fall (1837), Melville got a job teaching in a school house near Pittsfield (Parker 1996, 117f.). It was a time-consuming, trying experience. His pupils were rowdy and even physically threatening, and at the end of the year, he had had enough and handed in his resignation (Robertson-Lorant, 63).

Just as Gansevoort's business was recovering from the losses sustained in the fire, the economy crashed. It was the Panic of 1837. This time the injury to his fur and cap business was fatal and Gansevoort had to dissolve it. Maria Melvill, seriously in debt, unable to pay rent or even her grocery bills was forced to move from Albany to the town of Lansingburgh, New York, a port on the Hudson River, where ships docked in the harbor and sailors frequented the town. Hoping to find a steady, remunerative profession, Melville enrolled in the Lansingburgh Academy, studied engineering, and received his Certificate as a surveyor and engineer in November 1838. His uncle, Peter Gansevoort

introduced him to William Bouck, one of the commissioners of the Erie
Canal, which was then undergoing extensive renovation, and Melville
applied for, but failed to get, a job. At the same time, Melville had begun
writing, and his first extended piece, "Fragments from a Writing Desk,"
appeared in the May 1839 issue of the *Democratic Press and Lansingburgh
Advertiser*.

But by writing, Melville could not solve the financial troubles the
family was facing, which Maria described on May 23, 1839, when she
wrote to her brother,

> I have been under the painful necessity of again borrowing
> from Mrs. Peebles besides something owing the
> Shoemaker. *Can you send me a remittance this week*. [*sic*] I
> think some plan must be resolv'd upon, or something
> decided about my support untill [*sic*] my Sons can do for me
> & relieve my mind from an unsupportable weight of
> uncertainty—Hermen [*sic*] has gone out for a few days on
> foot to see what he can find to do—Gansevoort feels well
> enough to go about, & will leave for New York in a few
> days. (Robertson-Lorant, 68)

Melville found nothing; moreover, the idea of office work, had he
found it, was repugnant to him. He thought it stifling and dull. With the
encouragement of his cousin Leonard Gansevoort, he decided to go to
sea and signed on to the *St. Lawrence*, a passenger cargo ship bound for
the English port city of Liverpool, as a hand. The boat was under way
on June 5, 1839. Melville washed decks and cleaned out pig pens and
chicken coops. Once in Liverpool, he was free to roam about, and saw
on its streets the underside of a rough city. The *St. Lawrence* returned to
the docks at South Street in lower Manhattan on September 30, 1839.

THE PERIOD BETWEEN MELVILLE'S SEA VOYAGES

Financially, things were no better for Maria Melvill when Melville
returned than before he left for Liverpool. Her brother Peter wrote
Lemuel Shaw on October 4, 1839,

> It is with the most painful feelings that I inform you, that by
> the failure in business, Some time since, of her son

Gansevoort, Mrs. Melville has become entirely impoverished—mortgages are foreclosing upon her real estate & as I have just heard, her furniture is now advertised for sale. (Parker 1996, 152)

Later that month Melville visited Uncle Peter with a letter from his mother begging for help. Uncle Peter wrote back that he was burdened with the debt from Gansevoort's failed business, which he had guaranteed. He complained moreover that their brother Herman Gansevoort (the uncle after whom Herman Melville was named) was not sharing in the cost of helping their sister. He ended by writing that, "Money has not for many years been more scarce than it is at present," but he enclosed a check for $50 (Parker 1996, 153).

Melville himself was able to give his mother enough money from his sailor's pay to save the furniture and with the rest he furnished himself with proper clothing for a job he got teaching at the Greenbush & Schodack Academy in East Greenbush, New York. Maria was hopeful; now her second son would be earning a salary, and Melville not only taught at the school but was apparently writing, for under the name of "Harry the Reefer,"—reefing is a nautical term indicating the act of taking in a sail—there appeared a sea story called "The Death Craft" in the November 16, 1839 issue of the *Lansingburgh Democratic Press and Advertiser* which Melville scholars believe he wrote.

In the interest of delivering the family from debt, Melville lived frugally, worked diligently, and around March 1840, learned that he would not be paid for his work and that the school was closing. After that he did some substitute teaching in the Brunswick Public School 7, and was not paid for that work either. He sought whatever kind of job he could get, but prospects for earning a decent living once again were grim (Robertson-Lorant, 79f.). He decided then to go west to seek his fortune, the way many easterners of the time were. He went to Galena, Illinois, where his Uncle Thomas Melvill Jr., his Aunt Mary, and his Cousin Robert had gotten a farm after Thomas failed to make a go of it back east. Melville hoped he might be a surveyor or a teacher, or a writer for newspapers. With his friend Eli Fly, whom he had met at the Albany Academy in 1831, he traveled west on foot, along the Erie Canal, then by steamboat, locomotive, stagecoach, and horseback.

Fortune was, however, no more favorable in Illinois than in New York or Massachusetts. The depression brought on by the Panic of 1837 had moved west, too, and Uncle Thomas was no more astute at financial management than his father had been. He was dishonest, in fact, and had been stealing from his employer, who dismissed him but forbore to press charges. Melville and Fly found no work. One of the schools in Galena had been shut down. The young men helped out on the farm, but soon made their way back east, Melville to his mother's poverty and debt (Robertson-Lorant, 82f.). But he did not stay in Lansingburgh. With Fly he went to New York City to look for work. They stayed with Gansevoort. Fly, trained as a lawyer and commanding a fine penmanship, found work as a copyist, a scrivener. Melville, with no such marketable skill, found none. He spent his days reading, particularly Richard Henry Dana Jr.'s book of sea adventures, *Two Years before the Mast*, and other books and newspaper pieces about whaling and shipping, and he determined he would go to sea again, this time on a whaler. With Gansevoort he went to New Bedford, Massachusetts, and signed on to the *Acushnet*.

THE YEARS IN THE SOUTH PACIFIC

To get to the South Seas from the east coast of the United States, the *Acushnet* sailed down along the Atlantic coast of South America, rounded Cape Horn at the tip of Argentina, on April 15, 1841, and sailed into the South Pacific. The whaler then sailed up the west coast of South America, docked at San Juan Fernandez, an island off the coast of Chile (and alleged to be the island where Alexander Selkirk, the real-life model for Robinson Crusoe, had been shipwrecked) and then continued up to the Galapagos, the islands off the coast of Ecuador and Colombia where, six years earlier, Charles Darwin had made the observations of flora and fauna he published in *The Voyage of the Beagle*. Melville later wrote about these islands, calling them the *Encantadas*, or the enchanted isles, following the mariners who named them such because the unpredictable currents around them made it seem like they continually changed position. On these stops, barrels of oil which had been obtained from whale hunts were sent back to New Bedford. The *Acushnet* had made its first successful whale hunt and collected oil in March 1841 off the coast of Brazil. (Besides hunting the whales, when a whale was caught, the crew on a whaler also extracted its oil on the ship, boiling off the oil from the blubber in huge iron caldrons, then cooling the oil and funneling it into wooden barrels.)

The *Acushnet* was commanded by Captain Valentine Pease, a harsh man who exercised his authority tyrannically. When, for example, the ship anchored off the tropical island of Tumbes for thirteen days to take on fruit and water, he forbade the crew to go ashore, fearing they would not return (Robertson-Lorant, 101). Indeed, his anxiety was not groundless, for many of the crew of the *Acushnet*, throughout its voyage, did desert, Melville being one. On June 23, 1842, in the harbor at the island of Nuka Hiva, one of the Marquesas, he jumped ship with Richard Tobias Greene.

The Marquesas is a group of islands "of volcanic origin" characterized by "lofty central mountain ridges, deep valleys cut by mountain streams flanked by precipitous cliffs [which] sweep down to the sea" and by "narrow strips of black volcanic sand beaches [which] form at the valley mouths; ... on flanking sides, sheer ridges plunge steeply into the sea." The soil is rich, the climate subtropical. The islands were "discovered" in 1595 by the Spanish adventurer Alvaro de Mendana, who, with his crew, killed 200 of its inhabitants before leaving. The next European to visit the islands, in 1774, was Captain James Cook. Although there was less blood shed on this occasion, Cook's visit was more disastrous for the island because it opened it up to the "outside world." Soon, whalers, merchants, missionaries, adventurers, and the French colonial government came, bringing with them alcohol, firearms, subservience, and diseases, including venereal diseases. The culture of the islands was destroyed and the population fell from around one hundred thousand in 1774 to two thousand in 1923 (*www.tribalsite.com/articles/marque.htm*).

When Melville arrived, the culture of the islands was still in place. The assault from without was just beginning. In a sense, Melville was a part of it, but not an agent of it. In *Typee* and *Omoo*, he chronicled the culture which would soon disappear. He also told, with the embellishment of fiction, the story of his brief stay on the island—which he made longer in the book than it actually had been. And he described the nature of the people, their habits and customs, and his interactions with them.

As he made his way through the mountains of Nuka Hiva, Melville injured his leg, and none of the native ministrations did it any good. He and Toby, after a few weeks, desired to leave. It seems, however, that the natives did not want them to, and although Melville and Toby were not treated like prisoners but like guests, the islanders were willing forcibly to prevent their departure. On the pretense of securing medical help for Melville, Toby set out for the beach on July 27, 1842, to find a ship and then to return for Melville. He found, he recalled in 1846, the *London Packet*, and signed on. He told the captain he had a companion and asked for "a boat and crew armed that we might go and release him," but the captain refused and told him that an "Irishman, who had resided on the Island for some time," and who had brought Toby to the ship "would have my friend on board the next evening." The *London Packet* sailed the next day without Melville, and Melville and Toby did not see each other again until July 1846, after *Typee* was published (Parker 1996, 216ff.).

On August 7, 1842, the *Lucy Ann*, an Australian whaling ship, stopped at Nuka Hiva. Like the *Acushnet*, it carried an embittered crew near rebellion. One of the crew, John Troy, who acted as the ship's doctor, deserted at Nuka Hiva with the ship's supply of medicine. Natives of the island caught and returned him to the ship. When Henry Ventom, the captain of the *Lucy Ann*, in need of crewmen, learned from Troy that there was an American sailor on the island (Melville), he exchanged trinkets with the natives for him. The Lucy Ann arrived in Tahiti on September 20, 1842.

At the time that Melville's ship arrived, Tahiti was under siege by the French warship, *La Reine Blanche*, and its commander, Admiral Du Petit-Thouars, had engineered a seizure of the island for France. Captain Ventom of the *Lucy Ann* kept his ship from docking and deprived the crew of shore leave, but since he had become ill, he was removed from the ship at Papeete, the capital. The disorder aboard the *Lucy Ann* was such that the British consul, a man named Wilson, ordered that the ship be brought into port and that most of the crew, among them Melville, be jailed as mutineers. Some were imprisoned on *La Reine Blanche*. Melville with some others, however, was brought to a very low security British jail a short distance from Papeete, where they were free to roam about the beaches of this beautiful island, and when a whaling ship, the *Charles and Henry*, came into the harbor, Melville was free to sign on, and he shipped out to the Hawaiian island of Maui.

Melville arrived in Maui at the port of Lahaina on April 27, 1843, went on to Oahu, and stayed in Honolulu. For a day or two, he was in hiding because, coincidentally, the *Acushnet*, the ship he had deserted at Nuka Hiva, docked in Oahu. Had Captain Pease discovered him, Melville could have been seized and forced onto the ship. Once Pease had sailed, Melville roamed about Honolulu, got a job setting up pins in a bowling alley (Parker 1996, 250) and then indentured himself to Isaac Montgomery, a shopkeeper, and worked for him as a bookkeeper and clerk in his store selling calico. On August 17, 1843, after breaking his contract with Montgomery's consent, Melville joined the United States Navy for "3 years or cruize," and went aboard the *United States*, which was headed to Boston Harbor (Parker 1996, 260).

Melville's observation of the harsh, military discipline practiced aboard the *United States* became the subject of *White Jacket*. He had seen the way men worked on whale hunts, and the disorder of poorly commanded ships; he had been among savages and cannibals who had an unmediated connection to nature and a vitality which had been smothered in the people of Europe and the United States, and he had witnessed nineteenth-century imperialism in the form of warships in the harbors of tropical paradises. On the *United States*, he encountered crowded living conditions, callous officers, and the brutality of corporal punishment, of flogging in particular. Although he himself was never flogged, when such punishment was meted out, he was forced, with the rest of the ship's crew, to stand at attention and watch another man be flogged.

Melville's travels provided him with material for his books, and the long stretches of idle time on the ocean gave him the chance to fashion the stories of his adventures as he sat up nights on deck with shipmates spinning yarns, shaping his adventures into narratives, and embroidering and embellishing events for best effect. In a letter to Melville written in 1861, Toby Greene recalled "the many pleasant moonlight watches we passed together on the deck of the *Acushnet* as we whiled away the hours with yarn and song" (Parker 1996, 194). But it may be that the most important story Melville came upon during his years at sea was not one he lived or told, but one he heard about and then read: "When I was on board the ship *Acushnet*," he wrote, "I first became acquainted with" the *Narrative of the Most Extraordinary and Distressing Shipwreck of the Whale-Ship Essex, of Nantucket; Which Was Attacked and Finally Destroyed by a Large Spermaceti-Whale* (Parker 1996, 192; 197). The account was written by Owen Chase, and by coincidence, after Melville had heard of it, the *Acushnet* encountered a ship called the *Lima* at sea, and they gammed. A gam, Melville explained in *Moby-Dick* is "a social meeting of two … Whale-ships, generally on a cruising-

ground; when after exchanging hails, they exchange visits by boats'
crews" (Ch. 53). During this gam, Melville met "a fine lad of sixteen or
thereabouts, a son of Owen Chase." Melville

> questioned him concerning his father's adventure; and when
> I left his ship … he went to his chest & handed me a
> complete copy … of the Narrative. This was the first printed
> account of it I had ever seen…. The reading of this
> wondrous story upon the landless sea, & close to the very
> latitude of the shipwreck had a surprising effect upon me.
> (Parker 1996, 196)

The shipwreck Melville refers to occurred when, on board the
Essex, November 20, 1820, Owen Chase saw "a very large spermaceti
whale" break the surface of the water, lie quietly, spout, disappear, and
then come "down for us with great celerity[.]" "I involuntarily," Chase
continued,

> ordered the boy at the helm to put it hard up, intending to
> sheer off and avoid him. The words were scarcely out of my
> mouth, before he came down upon us with full speed, and
> struck the ship with his head, just forward of the fore-chains;
> he gave us such an appalling and tremendous jar, as nearly
> threw us all on our faces. The ship brought up as suddenly
> and violently as if she had struck a rock, and trembled for a
> few seconds like a leaf.

The whale was not finished, however:

> He was enveloped in the foam of the sea … and I could
> distinctly see him smite his jaws together, as if distracted with
> rage and fury. He remained a short time in this situation, and
> then started off with great velocity, across the bows of the
> ship, to windward…. I turned around, and saw him about one
> hundred rods directly ahead of us, coming down apparently
> with twice his ordinary speed, and to me at that moment, it
> appeared with tenfold fury and vengeance in his aspect. The
> surf flew in all directions about him, and his course towards
> us was marked by a white foam … which he made with the

continual violent thrashing of his tail; his head was about half out of water, and ... he came upon, and again struck the ship.

Captain Pollard and crew abandoned the sinking ship, gathered what provisions they could, and took to the ocean in three lifeboats, which soon got separated from each other. After supplies were exhausted, heat, starvation, and thirst took their toll upon the men in Pollard's boat. For food they determined to eat the flesh of those shipmates with them who had died:

> We now first commenced to satisfy the immediate craving of nature from the heart, which we eagerly devoured, and then eat sparingly of a few pieces of the flesh; after which, we hung up the remainder, cut in thin strips about the boat to dry in the sun: we made a fire and roasted some of it, to serve us during the next day

Once no carcasses were left to cannibalize, the men drew lots to see who would be killed to be eaten, and they proceeded in that way until they were rescued by the Nantucket whale ship, *Dauphin*. Owen Chase and his companions were rescued by the *Indian*, an English brig (Parker 1996, 195ff.).

MOBY-DICK AND NATHANIEL HAWTHORNE

The *United States* sailed into the Charleston Navy Yard in Boston on October 3, 1844, and within a few days, Melville was on land and his career as a sailor was at an end, *pace* the several long sea voyages he was to take as a passenger in later years. More significant than the actual voyages he had just completed, however, were the voyages in his mind he now began as he repeated the voyages of the last three years by writing about them. His habit of telling stories about his adventures was not confined to the decks of ships. Apparently he regaled his family with his narratives, and it was with their encouragement—although they regretted it later—that he took to writing them down (Parker 1996, 354).

In *Typee* and *Omoo*, he sought to give the impression that his fictions were actual true-life accounts. But he began, in *Mardi*, to assume the role of a writer who sought truth not in the authenticity of the details of his stories or by creating an imitation of real events but through constructing an imaginary narrative which could reveal philosophic truths of human experience symbolically and satirically. He became interested in the play of the mind, in exploring the possibilities of vision. *Mardi* was as much indebted to Melville's learning and to his intellectual penetration as it was to his exotic experiences.

After the popular success but the relatively poor commercial performance of *Typee* and *Omoo*, and after the critical attacks on him for their presumed departure from realism and for their sometimes theologically and sexually subversive content, Melville dedicated himself to writing, in *Mardi*, a book not intended to conciliate his detractors but to give scope to his growing literary, philosophical, and intellectual ambition. He had faith that *Mardi* would show him to be a "thought-diver" (Parker 1996, 617f.). His English publisher, John Murray, however, refused the terms Melville demanded, but Richard Bentley, another British publisher, agreed, despite the fact that his reader gave an account which ought to have made him wary. "There is such form of language ... such a prodigality of description—such a vivid picture of things that may be, however extraordinary,—that I began to hope, nay, to assure myself,—that now at last there was a book whose publication I could confidently urge." There was, however, a "but" to follow, and the reader found that after the "first third of the work," which seemed to have been written in order "to seduce the reader into reading the rest.... the work does not turn out to be what ... he had a right to expect.... I fancy not one in a score will discover what it's all about." He wrote the book seemed "to have been written by a madman," and that, in places, it was "quite delirious" (Parker 1996, 619).

Reviews of *Mardi* did not have the venom, when they were negative, that the reviews of Melville's earlier books had, primarily because reviewers did not have to focus on the disturbing aspects of the book's content but on the problem of figuring out what the content of the book was. There were reviews which praised Melville's writing, thought, wit, and allegorical fable, and there were reviewers who longed for him to return to writing travel adventure stories. But whatever the reviews, commercially the book was a huge failure.

Melville responded in two ways—1) by justifying *Mardi* to his English publisher, Bentley, who would lose quite a bit of money on it, saying that rather than "write a work ... calculated merely to please the general reader, & not provoke attack.... some of us scribblers ... always have a certain something unmanageable in us, that bids us to do this or that, and be done with it—hit or miss" (Parker 1996, 636). And 2) he set out to write for his next book, a far more commercial book—"a plain, straightforward, amusing narrative of personal experience—the son of a gentleman on his first voyage to sea as a sailor—no metaphysics, no conic sections, nothing but cakes & ale"(Parker 1996, 638). It would be a fictionalized account of his first voyage, the one he took when he was twenty, in 1839, to Liverpool, *Redburn*. And for the early chapters, he searched through the memories of his youth for material. In *Redburn*, too, Melville could insert events to underscore his abhorrence of American racism and growing anti-immigrant nationalism.

Melville did not like the book, but he was proud of himself for having written it in just two months, and after he wrote it, he quickly produced another work, *White Jacket*, or *The World in a Man-of-War*, which he intended, like *Redburn*, simply to be a pot boiler. About both books he wrote his father-in-law:

> For *Redburn* I anticipate no particular reception of any kind.
> It may be deemed a book of tolerable entertainment;— it
> may be accounted dull.—as for the other book, [*White Jacket*]
> it will be sure to be attacked in some quarters. But no
> reputation that is gratifying to me, can possibly be achieved
> by either of these books. They are two *jobs*, which I have
> done for money- being forced to it, as other men are to
> sawing wood…. Being books, then, written in this way, my
> only desire for their "success" (as it is called) springs from my
> pocket, & not from my heart. So far as I am individually
> concerned, & independent of my pocket, it is my earnest
> desire to write those sort of books which are said to "fail."
> (Parker 1996, 650)

It was an act of hubris to utter such words, for the gods were listening and they were, ever after, obliging, beginning with his very next book, *Moby-Dick*.

Before he could begin to concentrate on *Moby-Dick*, however, Melville had to find an English publisher for *White Jacket*, and decided to take the book to England himself rather than to entrust it to an agent. He intended not only to do the business of hawking the book but to give himself a vacation after writing three books in two years. His financial situation had improved. *Redburn* was selling well, and Harper's had advanced him $500.00 on *White Jacket*. Bentley owed him 100 pounds for *Redburn*, and Judge Shaw lent him money—essentially a gift—for the trip. Lizzie, the mother of a new baby, Malcolm Melville, born February 16, 1849, stayed in Boston with her parents, the baby, and his nurse (Robertson-Lorant, 213f).

Melville left for England October 11, 1849, on the *Southampton*, not as a sailor but as a passenger with a private stateroom with "plenty of light & a little thick glass window in the side." The first morning "by way of gymnastics," he climbed the rigging, and when gale winds and heavy rains made the ship pitch and roll and caused most of the passengers to be sea-sick, Melville felt fine. With friends he made on board, he spoke about philosophy and played shuffleboard (Robertson-Lorant, 217f.). In England, Melville visited several publishers, and succeeded only with Richard Bentley, who had published his last several books. He sold him *White Jacket* for two hundred pounds. After seeing London sites, both grand, like St. Paul's Cathedral, and squalid, like its poverty and public executions, Melville traveled to the Continent, going through Brussels, Liège, Aix-la-Chapelle, and the Rhine Valley. He saw the sights in Paris and returned to London. Homesick for his wife and family, he turned down an invitation from the Duke of Rutland to visit Belvoir Castle (pronounced "beaver") though he was eager "to know what the highest English aristocracy really & practically is," and sailing on the *Independence*, arrived in Manhattan January 31, 1850 (Robertson-Lorant, 231f.).

His reputation was somewhat recovered by the mostly favorable reviews the critics on both sides of the Atlantic gave *White Jacket* and the acknowledgement they extended him as a craftsman. What controversy there was over the book involved the issue of flogging, and while most reviewers were unable to go as far as Melville and support an end to flogging, most agreed that it was a practice which had to be subject to severe scrutiny (Parker 1996, 713ff.).

Melville, however, was less concerned with the reviews or his reputation than with the work which lay ahead of him. He had plotted out much of *Moby-Dick* on his voyage back to New York, and began work in earnest once he was home. Between February and June he secluded himself most of the time in his New York residence, relying on his own experience and a great deal of reading to create his metaphysical, encyclopedic, epic adventure-morality tale. In July 1850, Melville and his family moved to Pittsfield, Massachusetts, in the Berkshire Mountains fearing New York's heat and the summer epidemics. He could continue to work on *Moby-Dick* but also get out and about in the countryside, rambling alone and going on picnicking expeditions with friends. On one of those expeditions, on August 5, 1850, he met Nathaniel Hawthorne just at the height of Hawthorne's fame, when *The Scarlet Letter* was published.

On the morning of August 5, Melville, his friend and the editor of *The Literary World*, Evert Duyckinck, and Cornelius Mathews, a New York writer and editor, met Oliver Wendell Holmes, novelist, poet, physician, dean of the Harvard Medical School, and father of a future United States Supreme Court justice, at the train station, and rode over to Eden Hill, the estate—designed by Frederick Law Olmstead, who designed New York's Central Park—of the Reverend David Dudley Field, rector of the Congregational Church in Stockbridge, Massachusetts, and the editor of the *History of the County of Berkshire, Massachusetts*. There they met, among others, Nathaniel Hawthorne, arriving in a carriage driven by his publisher, James Fields.

The group took shelter under a large overhanging rock when a storm interrupted their outing and they drank champagne, which Dr. Holmes had brought along, and it was during these two hours of inclemency that Melville and Hawthorne began a conversation that brought them close and provoked the usually reserved Hawthorne to invite Melville to come the next day to visit him in the cottage nearby, where he was living with his wife, Sophia, and their children. Both Melville and Hawthorne were in exuberant spirits for the rest of the day. Melville "bestrode a peaked rock, which ran out like a bowsprit, and pulled and hauled imaginary ropes," and Hawthorne "called out facetious warnings that imminent destruction awaited them all," as they scampered among cleft and jagged rocks (Parker 1996, 745; 747).

During this excursion, too, Holmes introduced as a topic of conversation the problem of whose writers were greater, England's or America's. That argument encouraged Duyckinck to invite Melville, later on that evening when they were alone, to write an essay on Hawthorne for *The Literary World*, but he did not have a copy of *The Scarlet Letter* with him. Melville, however, did have a copy of Hawthorne's *Mosses from the Old Manse*, a collection of stories published four years earlier, which his Aunt Mary had given him upon his arrival in the Berkshires, and Melville took a few days away from *Moby-Dick* and wrote "Hawthorne and His Mosses," which appeared in two parts, on August 17 and August 24, 1850, in *The Literary World*.

The article was signed "By a Virginian Spending July in Vermont," rather than with his name so that neither Hawthorne nor Sophia, nor anyone else, knew it was Melville who wrote the essay. Melville chose that particular signature, however, not so much to hide himself as to distance himself from both the New York and the Boston literary circles. For the New York critics, Washington Irving (author of *The Legend of Sleepy Hollow*) was the supreme American writer, a point of view Melville held in contempt, judging Irving to be a "popular and amiable writer ... good, and self-reliant in many things [who] perhaps owes his chief reputation to the self-acknowledged imitation of a foreign model and to the studied avoidance of all topics but smooth ones." Melville equally contemned Boston critics, for whom Hawthorne was "a pleasant writer, with a pleasant style,—a sequestered, harmless man, from whom any deep and weighty thing would hardly be anticipated—a man who means no meanings." Hawthorne, as Melville saw him, was an American Shakespeare, not patterning his work on European models or avoiding the tragic depths of the American experience: "You may be witched by his sun light,—transported by the bright gildings in the skies he builds over you;—but there is a blackness of darkness beyond" (Robertson-Lorant, 249f.). It is clear now that speaking of Hawthorne, Melville was describing his own intentions as a writer as well.

Sophia Hawthorne, who saw the article when the poet, Henry Wadsworth Longfellow sent it to Hawthorne with commendation for the critic, wrote Duyckinck that the "ardent Virginian [was] the first person who has ever in *print* apprehended Mr. Hawthorne." And she wrote to her sister of "the Virginian" that "[t]he freshness of primeval nature is in the man, & the true Promethean fire is in him. Who can he be, so fearless, so rich in heart, of such fine intuition?" (Robertson-Lorant, 252)

While Sophia was praising Melville for his appreciation of her husband, although she did not yet know who he was, Hawthorne was appreciating Melville—knowing who he was—for his own books. He read them "on the new hay in the barn ... with a progressive appreciation of their author," saying of *Mardi*, that it was "a rich book, with depths here and there that compel a man to swim for his life." Hawthorne had Melville's books because Melville had delivered them to him, without knowing that he was, when he brought Hawthorne a package Duyckinck had sent him to give to Hawthorne along with a dozen bottles of champagne and a box of cigars he sent Melville for himself after he wrote the review (Robertson-Lorant, 251).

Melville visited the Hawthornes for a few days after Nathaniel Hawthorne's invitation, on the third of September 1850, and during the visit revealed that he was the Virginian who had written about Hawthorne in *The Literary World*. Melville spent time with Hawthorne and Sophia together and had long conversations with each alone. Sophia described Melville as "earnest sincere & reverent, very tender & *modest*." And despite the unlikeness of his facial features to her husband's, she admired him:

> He has very keen perceptive power, but what astonishes me is that his eyes are not large & deep—He seems to see every thing very accurately & how he can do so with his small eyes, I cannot tell. They are not keen eyes, either, but quite undistinguished in any way. His nose is straight & rather handsome, his mouth expressive of sensibility & emotion— He is tall & erect with an air free, brave & manly. When conversing, he is full of gesture & force, & loses himself in his subject—There is no grace nor polish—once in a while his animation gives place to a singularly quiet expression out of these eyes, to which I have objected—an indrawn, dim look, but which at the same time makes you feel—that he is at that instant taking deepest note of what is before him—It is a strange, lazy glance, but with a power in it quite unique—It does not seem to penetrate through you, but to take you into himself. (Parker 1996, 773)

Melville also took afternoon walks with Hawthorne. Melville told Sophia, she wrote, that although he [Melville] was usually a silent man, "he found himself talking to Mr. Hawthorne a great deal," explaining that "Hawthorne's great but hospitable silence drew him out" (Parker 1996, 776). Indeed, in his essay, Melville had written that Hawthorne "dropped germinous seeds into my soul.... He expands and deepens down the more I contemplate him" (Parker 1996, 755). That was the effect which being in his presence had on Melville, too. He left Hawthorne even more deeply resolved and inspired to make *Moby-Dick* the kind of book Hawthorne's influence demanded, the kind he described in his essay when he described Hawthorne's work. And he was also determined to quit New York City and live as Hawthorne lived, near him in the Berkshires.

With $3,000 from Lizzie's father, Lemuel Shaw, and two mortgages, one for $1,500 and one for $2,000, Melville bought one hundred and sixty acres of land and a big house on it in Berkshire County. It was the sort of thing his father would have done, risking a purchase and putting himself in debt with no real resources of his own to support it, living on expectations—the sale of the lease on his New York residence and the success of *Moby-Dick*—rather than on real income. When the money from the sale of the lease did not materialize, Melville borrowed $2,050 at nine percent interest from his friend Tertulius Stewart, who owned a sugar refinery, without telling Lizzie. He called the place "Arrowhead" because of the Indian artifacts he found there. He actually did farm work, too, besides writing, and he chopped wood. In town, he made friends and talked politics, arguing especially whether the anti-slavery position ought to take the form of absolute immediate abolitionism or an effort at compromise toward the slow elimination of slavery. Melville, at the time, took his father-in-law's position for compromise, believing its political necessity—protecting the Union—trumped even his own absolute moral opposition. Among his town friends was Joseph Edward Adam Smith, a staunch abolitionist, who later became Melville's first biographer.

The winter of 1850–1851 was a dizzying time for Melville. He was finishing *Moby-Dick*, which was growing in size and depth. He was taking up residence on a farm of his own where he would write and work outdoors. He was heaping upon himself debt and the anxiety which accompanies it. And he was visiting and conversing with Hawthorne, who was himself finishing his gothic, American romance, *The House of the Seven Gables*. And that was causing Melville to begin to imagine that his next book after *Moby-Dick* would be an American gothic, domestic romance, not a sea saga.

As with his previous books, *Moby-Dick*, published in England on October 18, 1851, was published there about a month before its American publication, which was on November 14, because of the lack of reciprocal copyright laws. Melville had sent his British publisher, Richard Bentley, corrected proof sheets of the book. Bentley, concerned that nothing blasphemous, sexually suggestive, or unfavorable to monarchy be included in the text gave *Moby-Dick* to an editor for a careful vetting, and the editor not only deleted so much that there were more than seven hundred discrepancies between the British and the American editions, but he also rearranged some of the text and removed the Epilogue in its entirety (Robertson-Lorant, 277). Without the Epilogue, it appears that everyone perished in the wreck of the Pequod—Ishmael, the book's narrator, too—and, absurdly, then, that a dead man was writing the story. It was that version of *Moby-Dick* which British reviewers saw and which they reviewed, and with which they found fault. In many instances, those reviews were reprinted in the United States, and despite the fact that American readers had the authentic text with the Epilogue showing Ishmael's survival and rescue intact, the British critics' responses to the book had great influence on American attitudes.

An especially important review appeared in the London *Athenaeum* on October 25, not only because of its thorough disdain for Melville's work, but because it was reprinted in nearly its entirety as an authoritative pronouncement in two prominent Boston papers, the *Post* and the *Statesman*, which then set the tone and were used as sources for similar excoriations in other papers. "The style" of *Moby-Dick*, the critic charged, "is in places disfigured by mad (rather than bad) English; and its catastrophe is hastily, weakly, and obscurely managed." Melville, furthermore, "must be henceforth numbered in the company of the incorrigibles who occasionally tantalize us with indications of genius, while they constantly summon us to endure monstrosities, carelessnesses, and other such harassing manifestations of bad taste as daring or disordered ingenuity can devise." The review ended with righteous castigation of the author himself, "Melville has to thank himself only if his horrors and his heroics are flung aside by the general reader, as so much trash belonging to the worst school of Bedlam literature,—since he seems not so much unable to learn as disdainful of learning the craft of an artist." To conclude, the writer in the *Post*, in his own voice now wrote that *Moby-Dick* "is not worth the money asked for it, either as a literary work or as a mass of printed paper" (Parker 2002, 18ff.).

There is some excuse for the critic in the *Athenaeum* for his bad review. He, after all, without knowing it, was not reading the *Moby-Dick* which Melville had written but the butchered version. But the Boston critic had in his hands *Moby-Dick* as Melville wrote it, with the all-important Epilogue intact. He, however, neglected to read the book for himself through to the end, and thus, by dereliction of critical responsibility, was unaware that Melville's was a different text from the British text, and that the British text was corrupt: "We have read nearly one half of this book," he admitted, and then reprinted lengthy quotations from the *Athenaeum* reviewer (Parker 2002, 18). Since Melville, at first, was unaware that the London edition of *Moby-Dick* had been disfigured, the reviews were perplexing to him except as confirmation of the intellectual and artistic isolation he already had come to feel was his fate.

Some later American reviewers were much more favorable to the book, especially George Ripley in the New York *Tribune* on November 22, 1850:

> We think it the best production which has yet come from the seething brain, and in spite of its lawless flights, which put all regular criticism at defiance, it gives us a higher opinion of the author's originality and power than even the favorite and fragrant first fruits of his genius, the never-to-be-forgotten *Typee*. (Parker 2002, 26)

Such a review, however, came too late, after the general attitude toward the book had been established, and even some of the good reviews had damning reservations. In *The Literary World*, in which Melville had written his profound homage to Hawthorne, his friend, Evert Duyckinck, the journal's editor, tempered his favorable review with criticisms he was "reluctantly compelled" to make regarding Melville's "bewildering, barren, and void skepticism [*sic*]" and his "running down of creeds and opinions." "We do not like to see," he wrote, "what, under any view, must be to the world the most sacred associations of life violated and defaced." And he particularly objected to Melville's tolerance for the cannibal Queequeg's religious devotion to his carved idol god Yojo (Parker 2002, 24).

The reviewer in the newspaper of the Congregationalists, the New York *Independent*, identified only as "H," asserted that in Melville,

> there is a primitive formation of profanity and indecency that is ever and anon shooting up through all the strata of his writings…. The Judgment day will hold him liable for not

turning his talents to better account.... The book-maker and
the book-publisher had better do their work with a view to
the trial it must undergo at the bar of God. (Parker 2002, 25)

One can only be left hoping that God is a better reader than this critic.

The unwelcoming reception of *Moby-Dick*—it was called "a
monstrous bore" by the *Southern Review*, for example—and the *ad
hominem* condemnations of its author guaranteed poor sales. Fifteen
hundred copies of *Moby-Dick* were sold during the month after
publication, 2,300 more copies were sold during the next eighteen
months, and 5,500 hundred additional copies over the next fifty
years. Melville's lifetime earnings on *Moby-Dick* were $1,260, and
Lizzie got another $81.06 during the fifteen years she survived her
husband.

The immediate negative response to *Moby-Dick* confirmed for
Hope Savage Shaw (Melville's wife Lizzie's step-mother) and Lemuel
Shaw Jr., (Lizzie's half-brother) the disdain they had begun to feel for
Melville as a man, a provider for his family, and a writer at the time
Mardi was published. Their judgment, indeed their wish, that Melville
would quit writing was spreading through the family, infecting other
members, Lizzie herself, in time, until late in her life when her husband
was restored to her good opinion, when his literary reputation began to
revive towards the end of his life and following his death.

PIERRE AND ITS CONSEQUENCES

Even after the disgrace of *Moby-Dick*, Melville was not finished with the
market place. Like his Ahab in frenzied and obsessive pursuit of the
whale, he drove himself—sometimes, it might seem, madly—to find
within himself, in the deep waters of his imagination, and to bring
under his linguistic control, that book which would vindicate his
pursuit, proclaim his standing as an artist, and bring him recognition
and fortune (Parker 2002, 49; 51). But what he brought up from his
divings seemed mostly to those who saw them to be monstrosities,
which, almost desperately, followed one another throughout the 1850s.
Pierre, Israel Potter, The Confidence Man, a series of long stories, even his
three-year stint as a lecturer were all undertaken seemingly in defiance
of the public as much as with it in mind, and his work was met with

little acceptance. Indeed, criticism of Melville's work continued to be criticism of Melville himself, as in these sentences from a review of *Moby-Dick*:

> Mr. Melville's vanity is immeasurable.... He will center all attention upon himself.... From this morbid self-esteem, coupled with a most unbounded love of notoriety, spring all Mr. Melville's efforts ... all his declamatory abuse of society, all his inflated sentiment, and all his insinuating licentiousness. (Parker 2002, 72)

No book could seem as different from *Moby-Dick* as *Pierre, or The Ambiguities*, yet the response to it was not so very different from the response to *Moby-Dick*. *Pierre* was taken to be the work of a crazy man. It is not an easy book to read. The language is stilted, florid, and sentimental, but purposely so in order to subvert stilted, florid, and sentimental attitudes by emphasizing them. Baroque plot elements include incest and murder. *Pierre* is a blend of the gothic novel popular at the end of the eighteenth and the beginning of the nineteenth centuries and the novel of sentiment often written by women and directed to a female readership. It relies on the legendary glory of a family's history—much of it Melville's own—and its hidden underside. In its psychological examination of bizarre family relationships, *Pierre* anticipates some of Sigmund Freud's formulations by half a century.

While Melville was mining his family history in the novel, the circumstances of his present immediate family were becoming deepeningly troubled. Financial difficulties, moodiness, and depression at his inability to win regard as either a serious or a popular novelist, and a furious and stubborn, but, nevertheless, all-absorbing involvement with the new book he was writing, were isolating Melville from Lizzie and destroying the vitality of their earlier connection.

In October of 1851, after a difficult pregnancy, Lizzie gave birth to their second son, Stanwix, named for the fort Melville's maternal uncle, Peter Gansevoort, had successfully defended in 1777. Melville's mother described Lizzie's condition after delivery:

> She is very nervous being constitutionally so, and now being so weak, with loss of appetite ... a sheet had to be placed on

the wall to cover the paper the figures of which seem'd to be
in motion. (Parker 2002, 31)

Lizzie's weakness was not the neurasthenic disturbance Maria Melville's
remarks might suggest, but a breast infection which spread and became
a sizeable and growing lump under her left arm and which caused severe
pain, especially when she nursed the baby. Thus husband and wife were
each in the throes of their own agonies and inattentive to each other.
Around Thanksgiving Melville took Lizzie to Boston. He left her at her
father's house to wean the baby and to be treated by the family doctor,
who applied poultices. Her healing was slow, and even at the end of
December, Lizzie wrote Melville that she was "suffering a good deal of
pain" (Parker 2002, 34).

When Melville took the manuscript of *Pierre* to the Harper
brothers in January 1852, they did not want it. Rather than flatly
refusing to publish the book, their strategy was to make him an offer he
could not accept. Rather than their former fifty-fifty profit-splitting
arrangement, they offered a contract which would give him twenty cents
on the dollar. Melville asked for some time to consider the matter and
went to Evert Duyckinck's office to consult with his friend, the editor of
The Literary World, who had good connections among publishers.
Duyckinck told him quite firmly that he could not recommend the book
to any publisher. Melville, on the strength of this rejection, accepted,
galling as it was, the offer from Harper's. When Duyckinck reviewed
Pierre in the August 21, 1852, issue of *The Literary World*, he wrote that
the book violated the "holy relations of the family." Melville severed his
friendship with Duyckinck for a number of years thereafter and
cancelled his subscription to *The Literary World* (Parker 2002, 77ff.).
Consumed with anger, Melville expanded *Pierre* adding a bitter satiric
subplot in which he casts Pierre as an author and vilifies critics and
publishers. Harper Brothers published the gothic romance as first
presented to them, not the augmented edition which included the
Harper brothers among the villains (Parker 2002, 88).

Richard Bentley in England, after informing Melville how much
he had lost on his previous books, declined to publish *Pierre*, and the
book was published only in the United States. Its reviews were terrible,
and again, Melville was personally abused as well as discounted as an
author, even to the point where his publishers at Harper, excusing
themselves for having printed the book by citing a binding contract and

their own over-generosity, suggested that "Melville is a little crazy" (Parker 2002, 124f; 131ff.).

Perhaps he was. He was bitter about his lack of success, driven in his work, sore in his body, irascible and moody with his family, riddled with debt, and medicating himself with alcohol (Robertson-Lorant, 370). But he continued to work, and he found a form of success in the early 1850s writing for *Harper's New Monthly Magazine*, and *Putnam's Magazine*, even earning money by doing so. For these publications, he wrote several of his finest stories, "Benito Cereno," "The Encatadas," and "Bartleby the Scrivner." For *Putnam's Magazine* Melville wrote the novel *Israel Potter: His Fifty Years of Exile*, a novel of a poor landless farmer who fights in the American Revolutionary War, afterwards goes to sea, has a series of adventures which reflect on the social and political scene, is exiled in London for fifty years, and finally returns to Boston where he is killed accidentally on the Fourth of July when a wagon veers from the road. It was first serialized in *Putnam's Magazine* and then in 1854, published as a book.

Alarmed at Melville's deteriorating health, which the family believed to be the result of his writing, Melville's mother tried, in 1853, to get him to stop writing by securing a government post for him. Nathaniel Hawthorne had been appointed United States Consul in Liverpool, now that Franklin Pierce was president of the Unite States. Pierce was a friend of Hawthorne's, and Hawthorne had written *The Life of Franklin Pierce*, his campaign biography. Maria Melvill's hope, therefore, was that Hawthorne might speak to the president and secure a post for her son. She also wrote to her brother Peter asking him to use his influence in Washington, explaining, "This constant working of the brain, & excitement of the imagination, is wearing Herman out, & you will my dear Peter be doing him a lasting benefit if by your added exersions [*sic*] you can procure for him a foreign consulship." Judge Shaw also became involved and along with the sea novelist Richard Henry Dana (*Two Years before the Mast*) attempted to get Melville a consulship in Hawaii, for which Melville, because of his great knowledge of the region, was a natural. But Melville lost that post to a dedicated party worker from New York. And even with the endorsement of James Van Buren, the vice president's brother, he was not appointed to a consulship in Antwerp, Belgium, either. Finally he was offered a post in Rome, but the pay for it was so little that it required a man of independent wealth to fill it (Robertson-Lorant, 327f.).

Melville finished his last novel, *The Confidence-Man*, a satirical, philosophical extravaganza full of cynicism and skepticism set aboard a Mississippi riverboat in 1856. It was not the book to revive his reputation or restart his career as an author. He found a small American publisher, Dix & Edwards, for it. They went out of business soon after its publication. None of this was of any consequence to his family, however. They were concerned more than ever about his health. Judge Shaw wrote to his son Sam,

> I suppose you have been informed by some of the family how very ill Herman has been. It is manifest to me from Elizabeth's letters, that she has felt great anxiety about him. When he is deeply engaged in one of his literary works, he confines him[self] to hard study many hours in the day, with little or no exercise, & this specially in winter for a great many days together. He probably thus overworks himself & brings on severe nervous affections.

Consequently, Shaw advanced Melville $1,500 from Lizzie's inheritance, and on October 11, 1856, Melville boarded the *Glasgow*, a propeller driven steam ship which reached Scotland a little more than two weeks later. There Melville began keeping a journal, which became his *Journal up the Straits* (Robertson-Lorant, 372ff).

EUROPE AND THE LEVANT, 1856–1857

From Scotland, Melville took the train to Liverpool, where Hawthorne was stationed, and the two spent several days together, taking walks, talking, drinking, and smoking cigars. Hawthorne's account of Melville at this time is important because he was not governed, in his observation, by the concerns or the resentments which influenced the attitudes of Melville's family:

> Herman Melville came to see me at the Consulate, looking much as he used to do (a little paler, and perhaps a little sadder), in a rough outside coat, and with his characteristic gravity and reserve of manner.... Melville has not been well, of late; he has been affected with neuralgic complaints in his head and limbs, and no doubt has suffered

from too constant literary occupation, pursued without much
success, latterly; and his writings, for a long while past, have
indicated a morbid state of mind....

Hawthorne described Melville as a man tormented by a private turmoil,
which revealed itself in an irresolvable conflict regarding faith and belief:

> Melville, as he always does, began to reason of Providence
> and futurity, and of everything that lies beyond human ken,
> and informed me that he had "pretty much made up his mind
> to be annihilated"; but still he does not seem to rest in that
> anticipation; and, I think, will never rest until he gets hold of
> a definite belief. It is strange how he persists ... in wandering
> to and fro over these deserts, as dismal and monotonous as
> the sand hills amid which we were sitting. He can neither
> believe, nor be comfortable in his unbelief; and he is too
> honest and courageous not to try to do one or the other. If
> he were a religious man, he would be one of the most truly
> religious and reverential; he has a very high and noble nature,
> and better worth immortality than most of us (Robertson-
> Lorant, 376f.).

The steamship *Egyptian* carried Melville from Liverpool south,
then east through the Straits of Gibraltar into the Mediterranean. After
stopping at Syra and Thessaloniki and then passing Mount Olympus,
where the gods of ancient Greece resided, the *Egyptian* docked in
Constantinople, now Istanbul, Turkey. Melville roamed the streets,
dizzied by the "great crowds of all nations" and "bewildered &
confounded with the labyrinth, the din, the barbaric confusion of the
whole." He was frightened by the "horrible grimy tragic air," and the
"rotten & wicked looking houses," where it seemed to him "as if a
suicide hung from every rafter" (Robertson-Lorant, 381).

From Constantinople, Melville boarded the *Acadia* for Alexandria.
He sailed through the Dardanelles, passed the plain of Troy, where the
battles of the *Iliad* were fought, passed Mount Ida and Sappho´s Lesbos,
and stopped at Smyrna where he admired the "ungainly" camels. From
Alexandria, he took the railroad to Cairo, which he called a "dust-
colored city ... nipped between two deserts." He was tormented by the
"multitudes of blind men" in the city's squares and by "the flies on [their]

eyes at noon." The intensity of the light in the desert overwhelmed him and made him think of the angelic light referred to in the *Zohar*, a mystical Jewish text. It moved him to write the poem, "In the Desert," whose last stanza shows his familiarity with John Milton's invocation to light at the beginning of the third book of *Paradise Lost*, "Bright effluence of bright essence increate":

> Holy, holy, holy Light!
> Immaterial incandescence,
> Of God the effluence of essence.

From Cairo, Melville went back to Alexandria, and from there he sailed to Palestine, landed in Jaffa, and with a Jewish guide made his way to Jerusalem. Passing through the Plain of Sharon, they stopped in Ramala, but Melville was restless and they left Ramala at two in the morning, crossed the desert by moonlight, and breakfasted in a cave near an ancient mosque at daybreak. By afternoon they had reached Jerusalem. Exploring the hills around Jerusalem, Melville met a party of tourists from Boston, and with them crossed the Plain of Jericho to Bethlehem. Melville stood on the mountain where Satan tempted Jesus, and he saw the Dead Sea. In Jerusalem, he offered "myself up as a passive subject, and no unwilling one, to its weird impressions." He "rose at dawn & walked without the walls." It was "a city pent in by lofty walls obstructing ventilation, postponing the morning & hastening the unwholesome twilight … besieged by [an] army of the dead." Parting from the city, he asked a question he might apply to himself as well as to Jerusalem, "Is the desolation of the land the result of the fatal embrace of the Deity?" And he concluded that if it were "Hapless are the favorites of Heaven" (Robertson-Lorant, 390).

From Jaffa, Melville traveled to Piraeus, the port of Athens, and from there to Naples. He visited Pompeii and saw Vesuvius, the volcano which consumed it. From Naples he traveled to Rome, where he spent three weeks wandering about, visiting museums, churches, gardens, and antiquities, and felt lonely (Robertson-Lorant, 394). In Rome too, he met Sam Shaw, Lizzie's brother, on the day he [Melville] was leaving for Florence. Originally it had been planned for the two to travel together starting at Liverpool, but Melville managed to avoid knowing his exact itinerary; the two had not met, and Melville had been free to be on his own. Melville continued through Florence, Venice, Verona, and Milan, then through Switzerland and Germany. He returned to London, visited Oxford, and on May 5, 1857, he left for the United States and docked in New York on May 20.

HOME, AGAIN, AND STILL AT A LOSS

Once back home, despite his long and varied excursion, nothing had really changed. *The Confidence Man* had been published April 1st, and despite its relatively laudatory reviews on both sides of the Atlantic, rather than gaining anything from it, Melville owed money to his English publisher, Longman's, as well as to his now defunct American publisher, Dix & Edwards. Lizzie's half-brother, Lem, true to himself, wrote his brother of the book that it belonged to "that horribly uninteresting class of nonsensical books he [Melville] is given to writing—where there are pages of crude theory & speculation to every line of narrative—& interspersed with strained & ineffectual attempts to be humorous" (Robertson-Lorant, 402).

Not surprisingly then, during his absence, Melville's family had begun planning how he ought to live once he returned. His sister, Augusta, wrote that by returning to "the sedentary life [of] an author writing for his support [Melville] would risk the loss of all the benefit to his health which he has gained by his tour, & possibly become a confirmed invalid. Of this his physicians have warned him." She hoped they could "induce him to lay aside his pen" if they had something ready for him to do on his arrival. Although their quest for political patronage had failed twice, that was the course they set upon again, seeking to get Melville an appointment to the Custom-House in New York (Robertson-Lorant, 401). They also thought he might be able to earn a living by giving public lectures. Melville did not want to lecture, but he told Lem Shaw that he'd be happy "to get a place in the N.Y. Custom House" (Robertson-Lorant, 403). He would, however, have to live in New York, and in July, Melville contracted to buy a house in Brooklyn near Flatbush Avenue. He put an ad in the Pittsfield papers to sell Arrowhead, his farm, but after several weeks with no interested buyers, he had to give up the idea of buying the Brooklyn house and the possibility of securing an appointment to the Custom House.

Melville was not a successful lecturer. In small social groups, on ship's deck at night, among family or friends, he was known to be a compelling talker who drew his auditors to him with his tales of his adventures. But on the lecture circuit he was far from ingratiating. He was distant and dull. Rather than speaking directly to his audiences about his own adventures and experiences, he read a prepared speech in a monotonous voice which sometimes made his auditors strain to hear. And his subjects were abstract. Rather than discussing *his* adventures, he spoke abstractly about the virtues of traveling. He presented philosophical discussions about the value of art and aesthetic analyses of Roman marbles. The problem was not that they were bad lectures. They weren't. But they were not what the public wanted. His lecture on the South Seas, for example, did not reflect the author of *Typee*, but a critical discussion of the wrongs of industrial capitalism and the transgressions by Christians against indigenous populations and their cultures. By 1860, Melville had had enough. He had not succeeded as a lecturer, and it is not surprising. He could not get himself to entertain his audience. It felt to him to be a form of prostitution (Robertson-Lorant, 403). From his three tours, over a period of nearly three years, he earned a total of $1,273.50 before expenses, substantially less than Ralph Waldo Emerson or Henry Ward Beecher (the father of Harriet Beecher Stowe, author of *Uncle Tom's Cabin*) were making as lecturers (Robertson-Lorant, 414).

What had become particularly interesting to Melville by 1860 was poetry—reading and, more significantly, writing it. Of course, there was no money in it, but by this time, Melville was entirely defeated financially. He could not earn a living and support a family by writing or by lecturing, nor could he procure a government appointment, and his health had suffered and he no longer had the vigor with which his youth had been blessed. Lizzie had the annual income from her father's investment and Judge Shaw supplemented that with enough financial help to support the family and Melville, too. He also paid off all of Melville's debts, except for the debt Melville had to Harper Brothers (Parker 2002, 416ff.). That one was particularly galling because it included charges for reprinting his books after the stock was burned in a warehouse fire in 1853.

In April 1860, too, seeing how badly Melville was doing, Judge Shaw encouraged him to sail with his [Melville's] brother Tom aboard the *Meteor*, of which Tom was the captain, to San Francisco: "I think," Shaw wrote Melville, "it affords a fair prospect of being of permanent benefit to your health, and it will afford me the greatest pleasure to do anything in my power to aid your preparation, and make the voyage most agreeable and beneficial to you" (Parker 2002, 416f.). He paid for Melville's trip. A sure sign that Melville was no longer the man he had been was that when the *Meteor* left Boston Harbor on May 30, 1860, Melville became "quite sea-sick," and suffered from "qualmishness" for more than a week afterwards (Parker 2002, 427).

Before he set off, Melville left with Lizzie a volume of poems he hoped to have published. She made a fair copy and sent it to Charles Scribner, who returned it, saying that "no doubt [the poems] are excellent," but he had recently published two other volumes of poetry and did not wish to commit the firm to "another venture in that line" when "the prospect is that neither of [the volumes he had already published] will pay" (Robertson-Lorant, 417). Lizzie tried another publisher and was met with rejection again. This collection of Melville's poems was never published, but it seems likely that many of the poems included in it were published later, probably in 1891 in *Timoleon*.

Melville returned home, cutting his trip short after Tom learned that he would have to haul cargo to England rather than sail to India, where Melville had planned to accompany him. Melville was homesick, too, and he'd written to Lizzie and his mother that "he has not experienced the full benefit hoped from the trip" (Parker 2002, 445). Shortly after his return, in early December 1860, South Carolina seceded from the Union.

Despite the impending national catastrophe, domestic, financial, and career woes were preoccupying Melville. He was writing poetry, but he was not making money, and he was essentially confining himself to his writing table and traveling nowhere beyond his imagination. Once again, therefore, he endeavored to land a consulship, in Florence or Glasgow, this time. Lincoln was now president, and the newly formed Republican Party was in power. Melville had not had luck securing a favor from the Democrats, but hoped that some of his Republican relatives might assist him. He traveled to Washington, D.C., saw the unfinished Washington Monument, the Capitol building without its dome, and went to a levee at the White House, where he stood in line and shook hands with Abraham Lincoln. But he did not get a government appointment. He was called back home, however, by the news that Lizzie's father, Lemuel Shaw, had died. With Judge Shaw's death, Lizzie inherited $15,000 and property, and the family became financially secure—so much so that they could rent an apartment in Manhattan for Melville and keep Arrowhead.

War and Poetry

When ocean-clouds over inland hills
Sweep storming in late autumn brown,
And horror the sodden valley fills,
And the spire falls crashing in the town,
I muse upon my country's ills—
The tempest bursting from the waste of Time
On the world's fairest hope linked with man's foulest crime.
Nature's dark side is heeded now—
(Ah! optimist-cheer disheartened flown)—
A child may read the moody brow
Of yon black mountain lone.
With shouts the torrents down the gorges go,
And storms are formed behind the storm we feel
The hemlock shakes in the rafter, the oak in the driving
keel.

—Melville "Misgivings," 1861

The author of *Typee, Omoo, Moby-Dick,* "Bartleby," and *Billy Budd* is not generally known as a poet, even if he is credited with having a poetic imagination and having written a rugged prose full of rich cadences. But for the last twenty years of his life, Melville's primary literary occupation was writing poetry. The poetry was essentially ignored during his lifetime, and it was hardly more appreciated when there was a revival of interest in his work towards the end of his life and during the first decades of the twentieth century, nor is his reputation as one of the giants of American literature, even now, based at all on his poetry. Like most of Melville's work, including much of his prose—nearly everything after *Omoo,* in fact—his poetry is difficult and demanding. It "proceed[s]" Alfred Kazin wrote, "from some grave meditative center," and is by turns "crabbed," compressed, and "full of wonderful lines" (Kazin 357f.). His epic, *Clarel,* runs some 18,000 lines, nearly nine hundred pages. The sonnet "Misgivings" provides a good example, however, of Melville's skill as a poet, the range of his diction, his control of metrics, and his ability both to express abstract thought in imagery and to compress his thought into poetic forms.

The Civil War provided the material for his first published book of poems, *Battle Pieces and Aspects of War*, released by Harper's after the war in 1866. The war became an emotional center for his thoughts to shape themselves around, for the Civil War brought Melville into contact with the world the way he had not been since the world had rejected him when his books, after *Omoo*, started to fail to gain acknowledgement and acceptance.

He had been a gradualist, like Judge Shaw, and tempered his anti-slavery position with the belief that for the sake of the Union the Southern states had to be placated. Therefore he supported laws he did not condone, like the fugitive slave act, which required the North to return runaway slaves to their masters. Once the war had begun, however, he was a dedicated advocate of the Northern cause. Unfortunately, his poor health, the bodily pain he suffered, made it impossible for him to fight in the war. From Pittsfield and New York City, he followed events and wrote about the course of the war in his poems. In the Spring of 1864, when his health had improved, Melville determined to observe the war directly and petitioned Secretary of War Edwin Stanton and Massachusetts Senator Charles Sumner for permission to visit a Northern encampment in Virginia. Permission was granted and Melville and his brother, Allan, arrived at a Union encampment in Virginia, south of the Potomac River. Security at the camp, which had been subject to Confederate raids was so lax that they just walked in. Melville was welcomed, however, and even rode out with a scouting party. After he returned to camp, he traveled to the headquarters of the Army of the Potomac and met General Ulysses Grant, who had known Melville's uncle, his father's brother, Robert, the man who had been discharged for stealing from his employer, whom Melville had visited in Galena, Illinois, with Eli Fly in 1840, after his voyage to Liverpool and before he set out on his three and a half year whaling adventure (Robertson-Lorant, 468ff.).

AN INSPECTOR OF CUSTOMS

The years after the war were years of public invisibilty as a writer for Melville, but not as a sociable man. Having exchanged residences with his brother, Allan now lived at Arrowhead and Melville's family now lived on Twenty-sixth Street in New York. Melville attended social gatherings, and there are even accounts of his lively and engrossing social conversation (Robertson-Lorant, 485f). Perhaps there was no better prelude to his literary withdrawal, besides the reviews of *Battle Pieces*, than the news Melville received at the end of May 1864, shortly after he returned from Virginia, that Hawthorne had died on May 19. Their intense but relatively short friendship marked a period of great hope for Melville as a writer, and Hawthorne, being the source of much of Melville's creative energy, was also the source of that hope. Now Hawthorne was dead, and so was Melville's career as a writer.

The reviews of *Battle Pieces* assured that. By this time in Melville's career, they have a haunting familiarity. There were, as always, a few good reviews, although always with near-damning qualifications. The critic in the *American Literary Gazette and Publishers' Circular* wrote that Melville "has abundant force and fire," and that "his words will kindle afresh the patriotic flame. But he has written too rapidly to avoid great crudities. His poetry runs into the epileptic." In *The Nation*, Charles Eliot Norton recognized that *Battle Pieces* contained "the rough ore of poetry," but added that "Nature did not make [Melville] a poet." In *Harper's Magazine*, his publisher's house organ, the poems were ranked "among the most stirring lyrics of the war." But in *The Atlantic Monthly*, William Dean Howells said the poems resembled "no poetry you have read ... no life you have known," gave no indication "that there has really been a great war, with battles fought by men and bewailed by women ... only ... Mr. Melville's inner consciousness has been perturbed." And in the *New York Times* of August 27, 1866, Melville was accused of "treasonous language" for a prose Supplement attached to the end of the volume in which he wrote that "those of us who always abhorred slavery as atheistical iniquity" must "forbear from measures of dubious constitutional rightfulness toward our white countrymen.... The years of war tried our devotion to the Union; the time of peace may test the sincerity of our faith in democracy" (Robertson-Lorant, 495f.). Post-bellum history has shown he was right in his warning.

The failure of his book of poems was a failure to regain viability in the literary marketplace, and once again, this time without his family's urging or assistance, Melville attempted to get a government appointment. He wrote to Henry A. Smythe, a banker he had met in Switzerland in 1857, who now, in 1866, was the Collector of Customs for the Port of New York. On December 5, 1866, Melville was sworn in as a customs inspector on the docks of Manhattan, a position he held for nearly the next twenty years, working six days a week.

Eighteen-sixty-seven was a desperate year for Melville and Lizzie, and the years which followed it remained bleak. Despite his having found a job, or perhaps in part because that job signaled the absolute sureness of his exile from the literary world, Melville's temperamental instability had not abated. He may have been violent with his wife. Lizzie was complaining to her family about their marriage. It may be, too, that their older son Malcolm became her emotional protector. There is little solid documentary evidence, but there are allusions in letters and family legends (Parker 2002, 640ff.). Ultimately, Lizzie did not leave Melville, but they did spend much time apart, she with her family in Boston and he in New York. But it may be that their discord had grave effects on Malcolm, or it may be that there were things in his life which are simply unknown to us. It is known that he kept very late hours, although both his parents believed that he nevertheless, remained sober and chaste, even if "frolicsome." Whatever may be the causes, on September 10, 1867, Malcolm, age eighteen, was found late in the afternoon locked in his bedroom, as if asleep in his bed with a gun in his right hand and a bullet in his right temple. He had not come down that morning when his mother called, although he had acknowledged the summons, and Melville had said to leave him alone, let him be late for work, and suffer the consequences. When Melville came home from his job that night, he broke down Malcolm's bedroom door and found the dead boy on his bed in a semi-fetal position. The inquest determined it was suicide, but after pressure from the family, the coroner emended the finding by saying Malcolm's death was by his own hand but undoubtedly accidental because, being a devotee of weapons, he slept with a gun under his pillow which accidentally went off as he reached for it. Melville and Lizzie endured the funeral with public, stoical restraint. There is no record of their private responses.

On April 4, 1869, Stanwix, eighteen, having inherited the Melville passion "to go to sea & see something of this great world," boarded the *Yokohama*, which was bound for Canton, China. In June, Lizzie left to spend the summer in Boston, and Melville was left alone in New York. Besides his work, he was reading Matthew Arnold's *Essays in Criticism*, and his underlinings in the book seem to indicate he was thinking about poetry and about literature as a career. Regarding poetry, Melville highlighted these remarks: "Genius is mainly an affair of energy, and poetry is mainly an affair of genius," and "It is comparatively a small matter to express one's self well, if one will be content with not expressing much, with expressing only trite ideas." Beside Arnold's comment that "The literary career seems to me unreal, both in its essence and in the rewards which one seeks from it, and therefore marred by a secret absurdity," Melville noted, "This is the finest verbal statement of a truth which everyone who thinks in these days must have felt" (Parker 2002, 674f.).

Life went on, year by year, unhappily for Melville and his wife. Both suffered illnesses and misfortunes, and both withstood them. Melville's brother Allan died in 1872. Melville's job was often in jeopardy, not least because of recurring scandals regarding corrupt customs inspectors and bribery, but Melville—unlike his father and his uncle—was known for his incorruptible honesty and rectitude:

> Surrounded by low venality, he puts it all quietly aside,— quietly declining offers of money for special services,— quietly returning money which has been thrust into his pockets behind his back, avoiding offense alike to the corrupting merchants and their clerks and runners, who think all men can be bought, and to the corrupt swarms who shamelessly seek their price;—quietly, steadfastly doing his duty, and happy in retaining his own self-respect (Robertson-Lorant, 530f.).

In November 1873, a fire in Boston destroyed five thousand dollars worth of property Lizzie owned there, which meant a loss of five hundred dollars a year income from the property. Stanwix, who had been wandering around the world, had suffered illnesses and shipwreck, and finally returned to New York, for the moment chastened in his desire to roam, and apprenticed himself to a dentist, but he had become too nearsighted for such a career and was going deaf. He wrote Hope Shaw, his grandmother, "Fate is against me," and sailed for California (Robertson-Lorant, 531).

In the midst of so much desolation, two positive achievements must be noted. The relation between Melville and Lizzie became easier and warmer, and Melville became absorbed in writing *Clarel: A Poem and Pilgrimage in the Holy Land*, the long, contemplative, philosophical epic centered on the conversations of a group of pilgrims making their way through the holy places and back alleys of Palestine. Its subject is the very spirit of the time and the search for faith in a materialist age and for a vision of organic knowledge which shows the interpenetration of matter and spirit, individual and society in a world where mechanistic knowledge was rending connections. *Clarel* was a project Lizzie worked on with Melville, rather than opposing his work as a writer. In the published edition of the poem Melville gave to Lizzie, he inscribed, "This copy is specially presented to my wife, without whose assistance in manifold ways I hardly know how I could have got the book ... into shape, and finally through the press." His uncle, Peter Gansevoort also was supportive and gave him $1,200 towards its publication before his death, and Melville dedicated the poem to him.

Melville planned *Clarel* for publication during the American Centennial. When Putnam did publish it in 1876, rather than being greeted as a defining contribution to the literature of the nation, and a meditation on American culture and values, it was shunned in America as bewildering, "something of a puzzle ... in design and execution." It had "no plot" and what qualities it had were "lost in an overwhelming tide of mediocrity" (Robertson-Lorant, 553f.).

Clarel was not published in England, but a few copies managed to get into the hands of reviewers, who were more appreciative than their American counterparts. The London *Academy* called it "a book of very great interest, and poetry of no mean order." The "rugged inattention to the niceties of rhyme and meter here and there," the reviewer suggested "seems rather deliberate than careless." The review concluded that "this interesting poem ... deserves more attention than we fear it is likely to gain in an age which craves for smooth, short, lyric song, and is impatient for the most part of what is philosophic or didactic" (Robertson-Lorant, 553). It got so little attention that in 1879, at Putnam's request, Melville signed a release allowing them to pulp the 224 volumes remaining of the 350 which had been printed.

THE LAST YEARS: TENDING HIS GARDEN

Herman Melville died in his sleep of a heart attack on September 28, 1891. His last years were often plagued by physical illness and by losses, but not entirely. His brother, Tom, who had captained the *Meteor*, on which Melville had sailed to San Francisco, died in 1884. His younger son Stanwix, who had never found himself or settled down, died of tuberculosis, in California, on February 23, 1886, at the age of thirty-five. His daughter Elizabeth suffered from arthritis so severe it made her an invalid. His daughter Fanny was more fortunate. She did marry—

Henry Thomas, on April 5, 1880—and gave birth to four daughters, two of whom were born early enough, 1882 and 1883, to be Melville's delights in his old age. He took them to romp in Central Park and sat them on his lap and told them stories (Robertson-Lorant, 579).

Melville seems to have achieved a certain quietude of spirit during his last years despite misfortune and much of the world's contumely by having mastered the sort of indifference to life's vicissitudes implicit in the words of the philosopher Schopenhauer which he underlined in his edition of *The World as Will and Idea*: "to die willingly, to die joyfully, is the prerogative of the resigned, of him who surrenders and denies the will to live" (Robertson-Lorant, 612).

He had not, during the last years of his life, however, given up writing. After the failure of *Clarel*, Melville continued to work as customs inspector through 1888, when he retired. He inspected ships and went over inventory lists mornings; afternoons he spent at his desk writing (Parker 2002, 850). In 1888, he privately published the book of poems called *John Marr and Other Sailors* and, in 1891, *Timoleon*. Lizzie had inherited a great deal of money and he had inherited some too, and they were financially comfortable for the first time in their marriage, so much so that Lizzie put aside $25 a month just for the purchase of books. Melville also began growing roses in the garden he had dug in the back yard and sent dried petals enclosed in his letters to friends (Robertson-Lorant, 571). His last book of poetry, just ready for publication at the time of his death, was a collection called *Weeds and Wildings Chiefly: With a Rose or Two*.

During the last few years of his life, Melville was able to get a preview of what his reputation would become in the next century, although it seems he took the buds of recognition with the same equanimity he had learned to take the blasts of condemnation. W. Clark Russell, writing in the September 1884 London *Contemporary Review* called *Moby-Dick*

> a medley of noble impassioned thoughts born of the deep, pervaded by a grotesque human interest, owing to the contrast it suggests between the rough realities of the cabin and the forecastle and the phantasms of men conversing in rich poetry, and strangely moving and acting in that dim weather-worn Nantucket whaler.

The reviewer likened it to a

> drawing by William Blake ... madly fantastic in places, full of
> extraordinary thoughts, yet gloriously coherent—the work of
> a hand which, if the desire for such a thing had ever been,
> would have given a sailor's distinctness to the portrait of the
> solemn and strange Miltonic fancy of a ship built in the
> eclipse and rigged with curses dark. (Parker 2002, 865)

In April 1886, a Danish artist, Peter Toft, made several water color
illustrations of Melville's work. And in 1886, Melville received a letter
from the English poet Robert Buchanan, saying, "Your reputation here
is very great. It is hard to meet a man whose opinion as a reader is worth
having who does not speak of your works in such terms as he might
hesitate to employ ... towards many renowned English writers" (Parker
2002, 889). In 1885 Buchanan had published verses praising Melville in
the London *Academy* and condemning his countrymen for not
recognizing his genius. And Melville was being read by men like William
Morris and George Bernard Shaw (Parker 2002, 898f.). Still, Melville
remained essentially unknown in his own land. In obituaries he was
called both Henry and Hiram instead of Herman, Melville, and often it
was written of him that "he had done almost no literary work during the
past sixteen years," since the publication of *Clarel* (Robertson-Laurant,
614).

So weak was his reputation in the United States at the time of his
death, that rather than offering it to a publisher, Lizzie took from
Melville's desk a sea novella he had been working on since 1888, *Billy
Budd*, and put it into a tin breadbox "for safe keeping." It remained there
until 1919, when Raymond Weaver, a Melville scholar and an early
biographer, who was in large part responsible for Melville's literary
resurrection, found it while going through his papers in the attic of his
house on Twenty-sixth Street in New York City (Robertson-Lorant,
593).

Melville was buried in the Woodlawn Cemetery in the Bronx
beside his son Malcolm. His headstone is a thick slab of rough granite
with an ivy border carved into the stone. His name and birth and death
dates are chiseled into the base of the stone. A carved scroll unfurls down
the front of the stone and was left blank.

Works Cited

Kazin, Alfred. "'Melville Is Dwelling Somewhere in New York.'" In *Alfred Kazin's America: Critical and Personal Writings*, edited and with an introduction by Ted Solotaroff. New York: HarperCollins, 2003, pp. 344–369.

Parker, Hershel. *Herman Melville: A Biography: Volume 1, 1819–1851*. Baltimore and London: The Johns Hopkins University Press, 1996, p. 941.

———. *Herman Melville: A Biography: Volume 2, 1851–1891*. Baltimore and London: The Johns Hopkins University Press, 2002, p. 997.

Robertson-Lorant, Laurie (Robertson-Lorant). *Melville: A Biography*. New York: Clarkson Potter, 1996, p. 710.

www.tribalsite.com/articles/marque.htm

RANDA DUBNICK

Melville: American Romantic

Today, Herman Melville is considered a great American writer whose work is indisputably part of the canon of world literature. But during his lifetime, Melville struggled for critical recognition and financial survival. Melville was penniless and reduced to borrowing money all his life. Periodically attacked by religious critics for criticizing and ridiculing missionaries in his first two works, *Typee* and *Omoo*, Melville's troubles continued through the publication of *Moby-Dick*. A portion of Melville's financial and critical troubles were caused by the fact that the English publishers 'lost' the epigraph to *Moby-Dick*, and British critics took him to task for not explaining why Ishmael, the narrator, was still alive to tell the tale—exactly what the missing epigraph makes clear. Melville's career spiraled downward from there, with harsh critical reception that made it hard for him to find publishers.[1] Many of Melville's works were written early in his life, between 1846 and 1851. For decades afterward, he wrote very little, and what he wrote was not well received, but at the end of his life, he wrote *Billy Budd*, published posthumously in 1925.[2] Since that time, Melville's work has not only found favor, but has become part of the canon of great American and world literature.

That Melville's work is both characteristically romantic and distinctly American can be seen in his best known writings, from the early work that first brought him into the public eye, to the works that have become literary classics. Melville's works express a particularly American version of the Romantic sensibility.

Melville has been called a Romantic writer[3]—influenced by poets such as Byron, Coleridge, and Wordsworth—for his views of nature; his interest in the exotic indigenous cultures; his use of the brooding, emotional hero (in *Moby-Dick* and elsewhere); and his elevation of individual freedom in the face of authority. Some of Melville's best known images are the most Romantic; Ahab, the brooding Byronic protagonist; the great power of nature that is not always benign (the whale, ocean, and whirlpool in *Moby-Dick*); and the fascination with exotic native cultures. Melville places this Romantic sensibility in the context of American content, setting, and attitudes.

Considering his background, it is not surprising that Melville's work combines a traditional Romantic sensibility with American attitudes and realities. Melville's family was French, and his politics were influenced by his family's connection with the French revolution. Additionally, his paternal grandfather was at the Boston Tea Party, and Melville's views were influenced by this as well. In the repeated theme of ship captains who are tyrannical, unfair, monomaniacal or worse, Melville's ideas about fairness, tyranny, and defiance can be seen[4]—ideas that have much in common with Romanticism. Jean-Jacques Rousseau's *The Social Contract* expressed the idea that man is good in his natural state but is corrupted by civilization, and that people have the right to individual freedom. Rouseau's ideas were very important to the French Revolution and to Romanticism in French literature and beyond. The innate goodness of human beings and the importance of individual freedom are highlighted in Melville's work, including *Moby-Dick*, *Billy Budd*, and *Typee*.

Melville also drew on the work of American writers. He felt a great affinity with his contemporary Nathanial Hawthorne, whose writings about New England are also in the Romantic tradition. In addition, Melville was also influenced by Emerson and his ideas about Transcendentalism, self-reliance, and Gnosticism.[5] Gnosticism emphasizes intuitive knowledge of the divine; holds to the idea that all of nature was created by God; and that the original Adam was divine because made directly by God and, before the Fall, was completely innocent.[6] As we will see, the influence of Emerson's ideas about transcendentalism and Gnosticism is evident in Melville's works.

Melville's literary use of the seafaring life lent itself to aspects of Romanticism. It expressed an interest in exotic places and the power of the natural world, while reflecting the importance of sea trade in American life, and raised important questions in American political philosophy. In 1841, Melville took a whaling ship to the South Seas, jumped ship and spent a month on the Marquesas Islands, an experience which became the basis for *Typee*. Melville also was involved in a mutinous situation on an Australian ship.[7] His life on board ships raised concerns about authority and defiance that were explored throughout his career, from *Typee* to *Moby-Dick* to *Billy Budd*.

Melville celebrates the diversity of the tribal cultures at a time of missionary zeal for conversion and colonialism. As already mentioned, his early works *Omoo* and *Typee* take to task missionary and colonial activity in both Tahiti and Hawaii (the Sandwich Isles). His interest in the exotic began with *Typee*, and continued not only in *Omoo*, but in his portrayal of the crew members of the *Pequod* in *Moby-Dick*. Melville's portrayal of indigenous, exotic, non-western cultures is consistent with a Romantic sensibility.[8] Similarly, works of French Romanticism which may have influenced Melville celebrate exotic natives, such as *Les Natchez* by Francois Rene de Chateaubriad, founder of French romantic literature. *Les Natchez* is based on a visit to the United States and purportedly on observations of American Indians (published in 1826, written between 1794 and 1799).

One key American Romantic theme found in Melville's work is his juxtaposition of the Christian European with indigenous non-Christian cultures. In *Moby-Dick*, Melville makes much of the close bond between Ishmael, the product of Western Civilization, and Queequeg, the New Zealand native, even suggesting that they are twins and soul mates, perhaps signifying that the differences between them are illusory. Melville creates large and generally positive roles for characters from indigenous or tribal cultures, while at the same time, he critiques the missionary spirit, the urge to colonize, and the narrow prejudices of westerners.

Further defining the American-ness of Melville's Romanticism is his use of American attitudes, ideals, and history. The setting and backdrop of *Moby-Dick* is New England and the novel reflects a time of American growth and an increased reliance on sea trade and whaling—presenting a picture of the United States at a particular time and place. In Melville's works, the juxtaposition of European and indigenous populations takes place offshore to a great extent, but nonetheless reflects a central issue repeated in American history—as well as in contemporary life. America is a country that is home to people originating from all over the globe. For example, in *Moby-Dick*, the *Pequod* can be seen as a kind of microcosm of the world order, as a kind of "melting pot" with all kinds of people on board. Although the action of *Billy Budd* takes place on board a British ship, the novel deals with issues of fairness, justice, tyranny, and the rule of law that reach far beyond the confines of the ship, and, in fact, are central ideas in American political thought. Themes of authority, rebellion, and defiance appear throughout Melville's work and many of the ship captains Melville portrays do not pass the standard of fairness for most Americans of any period. (At first view, it might seem preferable to go to sea with Captain Vere rather than with Captain Ahab, but a sailor could find himself in fear for his life with either choice.)

Finally, Melville's works are also Romantic in structural terms. Although to some degree, this may have to do with the financial pressures Melville was under—pressures to publish, and to quickly get the pages off to the printer[10]—his use of loose, organic, almost biomorphic structure that seems to grow almost on impulse and is sometimes not pruned[11] reflects a Romantic sensibility rather than a classical structure emphasizing balance and reason.[12]

TYPEE AND OMOO

Melville's early works, *Typee* and *Omoo*, share elements of Romanticism, especially the interest in and celebration of the "savage," the non-western, indigenous cultures; and both contrast this view of indigenous cultures with the ridiculousness of the rule-bound missionaries trying to convert the savages.

Both *Omoo* and *Typee* are about the tropics, Fiji and Hawaii respectively, and both grew out of Melville's early experiences as a "travel writer," and his observation of missionaries in those locations. Melville himself takes the role of protagonist of *Typee*, and tells a tale based on his month-long experience living in the South Seas after he jumped ship. Much of the humor of both *Typee* and *Omoo* comes from the juxtaposition of the indigenous and the European cultures, and the humor is directed at both sides. Melville satirically attacks the missionary zeal that too often lead to brutality and injustice against the "savages," while he celebrates the life of the indigenous peoples. Unfortunately for Melville, this unflattering portrayal of missionaries led to attacks by religious critics.[13] These two early works have a role to play in his Romanticism as he explores cultures distant not only in space but also in time, visiting cultures that seem to belong to a tribal era long before the modern age.[14]

Some of the themes characteristic of Melville's better-known and later works are already present in *Typee*—primarily the impulse toward mutiny and the impossibility of achieving it. Eventually, shipboard life under a tyrannical captain and the resulting conflict with authority lead narrator/protagonist Melville and his companion Toby to run away when the ship is docked on a tropical island.

Another prominent theme explored in this early work is the fascination with tattooing and writing. This fascination demonstrates an awareness of and an interest in language that might naturally be associated with exotic travel and piqued by exposure to indigenous cultures with strange languages as well as less familiar forms of communication such as tattoos, hieroglyphics, and carvings (not to mention the Babel that was the fishing or merchant ship). This interest in language is a theme that ultimately flourishes in *Moby-Dick*.

MOBY-DICK

Melville's masterpiece, *Moby-Dick*, epitomizes American Romanticism in its view of nature; in its interest in exotic, indigenous peoples; in the portrayal of the brooding Ahab, and in its attitudes towards authority and defiance as examined in the relationships of Ahab and the crew of the *Pequod*. In its particularity, *Moby-Dick* is about the defiant, possibly mad captain of one whaling ship who seeks revenge against a whale. In the larger sense, it is about man defying nature, trying to make sense of life and the powers in the universe that seem bent on human destruction. *Moby-Dick* is also an epic in its impulse to be both encyclopedic and universal.

Though the novel is quite complex, the main action can be summarized easily. Ishmael, a schoolteacher, decides to go to sea to cure his December melancholy, and after a random meeting with Queequeg, a tattooed New Zealand harpooner, Ishmael and Queequeg set out to sea together on the *Pequod*. Ahab, the ship's Captain, is intent on pursuing Moby-Dick, the white whale that maimed him on an earlier voyage, resulting in the loss of his leg. After Ahab's repeated discussions with first-mate Starbuck, and after encounters with several other ships, the *Pequod* finds Moby Dick and gives chase for three days. Predictably, nature wins out as Moby-Dick brings the whole ship down, and the *Pequod* breaks apart and is sucked into a whirlpool; Ahab watches as he drowns, strangled by his harpoon rope. The lone survivor, Ishmael, floats in a canoe-shaped coffin, fashioned during the sea voyage for his friend Queequeg who had fallen ill, but recovered. After floating for a day and a half, Ishmael is picked up by the ship *Rachel*, and is the only survivor left to tell the tale.

With its reflections on the particular position of the United States, most notably the American race, to conquer the wild frontier, *Moby-Dick* exhibits a uniquely American sensibility. Set in a time of great international trade[15] when much of American literature is focused on conquering the frontier and its indigenous peoples, Melville looks to the sea to explore another kind of frontier, where the whalers, like their westward bound counterparts, are out to subjugate nature. Though much of America's wealth would be found in the nearly inexhaustible natural resources found west of the original colonies, a good deal of America's importance was built through the trade based on life at sea, and although it is not dealt with by many American writers, it was as important a part of American history frontier life, the cowboy or the Gold Rush.[16] Furthermore, one should consider that the diversity reflected in the characters aboard the *Pequod* is not only a reflection of the reality of life on the whaling ships of the time, but also a reflection of what came to be an ideal of American life—perhaps making Melville's tale all the more universal. (Contrast *Moby-Dick* with Charles Dickens's novels in which all the characters are English, or even Hawthorne's work, in which all the characters are New England Puritans.) In this respect, Melville is more like Shakespeare, who populated his dramatic world with Moors, Italians, Danes, and Scots.

Ultimately, *Moby-Dick* is American in its setting with the first third of the novel taking place in New England, before Ishmael and Queequeg head out to sea. Within the first two chapters, Melville includes African Americans (in the church in Bedford) and refers to American Indians as the first whale hunters. When Ishmael and Queequeg board the *Pequod*, the reader sees not just an American whaling ship but a microcosm of the world, with international characters representing many cultural, philosophical, and religious points of view.

Still, the story of *Moby-Dick* is Ahab's story—a great man who has become irrationally focused on his quest to exact revenge but ultimately loses his life and the lives of his crew. Ahab can be seen as a tragic figure like Oedipus or Othello, a heroic figure who does great damage.[18] Ahab's greatness is his charismatic leadership and courageous defiance, but he leads in the wrong direction. He is tragic in that he appears fated to chase the whale following his unfortunate, but random, maiming. In the chapter called "The *Pequod* Meets the Samuel Enderby," Ahab's response to his personal situation is juxtaposed with that of another ship captain who has lost an arm to Moby-Dick, but unlike Ahab, hasn't laid chase, saying instead that Moby Dick is "welcome to the arm he has, since I can't help it, and didn't know him then, but not to another one. No more White Whales for me. There would be great glory in killing him, I know that; and there is a ship-load of precious sperm in him, but hark ye, he's best let alone; don't you think so captain" (p. 340). Ahab, impatient to find Moby-Dick, shoves this captain out of the way, who then whispers to Fedallah, "Is your captain crazy?" (p. 340). Thus, this important encounter serves as a corrective, reminding readers that there are alternatives to Ahab's response to his situation.

The *Pequod* has several encounters with other ships, and something is revealed with each encounter, often highlighting something about Ahab as he is juxtaposed with other captains and other choices. For example, much is learned about Ahab's character when he refuses to help the captain of the ship *Rachel* search for his son as well as the young son of his friend—both of whom have been lost at sea (Ch. 128). This encounter makes clear Ahab's single-minded pursuit of vengeance which leaves no room for concern for the tragedy of others.

Some critics have interpreted the story of Ahab's vengeance and destruction in a traditional Judeo-Christian context. Is Ahab punished for his failure to forgive or for ursurping the vengeance of the Lord as his own? Is he to be compared to Jonah or Job?, The quotations at the beginning of *Moby-Dick*, assembled by the fictitious sub-sub-librarian for Ishmael, include Biblical references to God preparing a big whale to swallow Jonah, conveying the idea that God can use such creatures for the punishment of mankind.[19] There is even a reference to Jonah in one of the first chapters of the novel; the innkeeper is named Jonah, and Ishmael talks about this (p. 27). If the logic of these parallels are followed, it is not only the whale that Ahab defies, but God as well, and the forces of nature behind the whale. By refusing to accept his situation, Ahab also defies his maiming and the authority of the unseen power behind that event. In that sense, he can be viewed as the tragic hero of antiquity, similar to Antigone,[20] thus moving the work out of a conventionally Christian context.

Interpreting Ahab's story in a strictly Christian context has its limitations, for few characters on the *Pequod* are western, and most of the characters are not Christian—Starbuck being a key exception.[21] The presence of the non-Christian characters forces readers to see this narrative in a more secular view. In fact, it has been suggested by Harold Bloom, among others, that seeing this narrative in a standard Christian context is an oversimplification, and that easy moralizing doesn't work.[22]

Furthermore, Ahab himself does not express traditional Christian beliefs. In "the Quarter Deck Chapter," readers get a sense of Ahab's religious ideas[23] as he expresses his belief in "some unknown but still reasoning thing" behind the "mask", and says that "all visible objects ... are but pasteboard masks" (p. 140). Ahab's religion[24] is expressed in "The Candles" when Ahab says, "Oh thou clear spirit of clear fire, whom on these seas I as a Persian once did worship, till in the sacramental act so burned by thee, that to this hour I bear the scar; I now know thee, thou clear spirit, and I now know that thy right worship is defiance" (p. 382). Melville has made the novel more universal by his substitutions of Ahab, a Persian converted from Zoroastrianism for a more conventionally "Christian" Captain, Peleg, as well as "pagan" New Zealand native Queequeg for a European westerner named Bulkington in the central role as harpooner.[25] These choices enlarge the context and make it more problematic to interpret the work solely under conventional Christian terms.

THE ACTION OF *MOBY-DICK*

Boiling the novel down to its comic book form is to focus on the action and lose much of the conflict. Consider that it takes 21 chapters out of a total of 135 before Ishmael and Queequeg board the *Pequod,* or that the denouement, the encounter with Moby-Dick, takes place in three very short chapters at the end of the novel. *Moby-Dick* is a novel that centers on the conflict over whether or not Ahab should do what he is set on doing. In a way, *Moby-Dick* resembles Hamlet, with discussion throughout the work about a proposed action, while the action itself is very concentrated and reserved for the end of the work.

The comic voice of Melville (or Ishmael) is evident early in the novel, for example in Chapters 3 and 4, "The Spouter Inn" and "The Counter Pane" in which Ishmael is to sleep in same bed as a yet unknown harpooner, and wakes up to witness Queequeg's entrance, tattooed all over his body and carrying a harpoon. In the morning, Ishmael wakes to find that the sleeping Queequeg has thrown his tattooed arm over Ishmael as if over a wife. Ishmael then describes the comedy of Queequeg parading around the room wearing only hat and boots, lying down beneath the bed to put on his clothes, and shaving himself with his harpoon. This is the stuff of broad comedy, and as in *Typee* and *Omoo*, the comedy is rooted in the juxtaposition of two cultures.

Ishmael and Queequeg spend a second night together, cementing their friendship with smoking and conversation in Chapter 10: "A Bosom Friend." The vocabulary of marriage and honeymoon continue to be applied to their warm feelings toward one another. The theme of pagan/Christian friendship is explored as Ishmael decides to befriend a pagan because his friendships with Christians have seemed hollow courtesy. To further the friendship, Ishmael decides to participate in Queequeg's idol worship, despite biblical prohibitions, and a note to the text explains how much this would horrify the Presbyterians who hated Melville's earlier novels. Ishmael describes himself as Presbyterian, but then asks why on earth God would be jealous of a piece of wood. Ishmael says that if he wants to convert Queequeg to Christianity, he will first participate in his pagan rites. Together, Queequeg and Ishmael smoke, worship idols, and seem intent on breaking as many biblical prohibitions as they can.

Ishmael and the reader get their first view of Ahab and their first insight into what Ahab is all about in Chapter 36, "The Quarterdeck." Ahab has been pacing and brooding all day, and finally calls everyone together, nails a doubloon up for anyone who spots Moby-Dick, and tells his men that this voyage will be dedicated to the revenge upon and killing of the white whale that maimed him. Using charismatic rhetoric, Ahab manages to get almost everyone excited enough to assent to this plan, all but the three mates: Starbuck, Stubb, and Flask. Starbuck argues first that Ahab is chasing an animal that hurt him out of instinct and second that the business of the ship is to make money hunting whales, a goal not served by chasing Moby-Dick:

"Vengeance on a dumb brute!" cried Starbuck, "that simply
smote thee from blindest instinct! Madness! To be enraged
with a dumb thing, Captain Ahab, seems blasphemous." (p.
139)

One might second Starbuck's question by asking why Ahab should wreak
vengeance on Moby-Dick, since Ahab was pursuing the whale when he
was maimed, and the whale was acting in the interests of self-
preservation. Given the treatment of whales at the time,[26] a modern
reader concerned about environmental issues would tend to see whales
as victims rather than villains.

Nevertheless, Ahab's answer to Starbuck's objection is that whether
the whale was a dumb agent of a natural force or the principle of the
action, he will seek revenge. Ahab describes the white whale as a mask
that covers the force which he will defy. It is chiefly Starbuck who serves
as the "voice of reason." He is an ordinary, non-heroic man whose
reasonable point of view and calm approach are completely ineffectual
against the force of Ahab's power and personality. Starbuck, along with
Stubb and Flask, form a kind of Greek chorus, able to comment on the
action and interact with the hero, but unable to have much, if any,
impact on the unfolding tragedy. The three western voices of Starbuck,
Stubbs, and Flagg are juxtaposed with the three exotic harpooners (New
Zealander, American Indian, African) that Ahab singles out when he says
that Starbuck, Stubbs, and Flagg are to be cupbearers to the three
harpooners, and presumably subservient to them (p. 142).

This trio of western mates is clearly not up to the task of defying
Ahab (possibly due to Ahab's charismatic effect on the rest of the crew),
but one can't help but wonder whether, had they a little of Ahab's
defiance, they could have prevented the coming disaster. To give
Starbuck his due, there is a moment when, in Ahab's cabin, Starbuck tells
his captain to abandon pursuit of Moby-Dick, and Ahab points a gun at
Starbuck and tells him to leave. As is made clear in *Billy Budd*, attempting
mutiny can mean risking one's life, so mutiny should only be attempted
when success is assured, and in the case of Moby-Dick, most of the
Pequod crew seems to be in favor of the chase. It is interesting that
among those same quotations at the beginning of *Moby-Dick* assembled
by the fictitious sub-sub-librarian are allusions to mutiny, reminding
readers that mutiny is a possible response to tyranny, as the narrator is
aware.

Despite objections, Ahab will take upon himself the vengeance against Moby-Dick, and Starbuck and the others will be forced to go along with Ahab, even to their doom. For his rebellious spirit and rejection of received truth, Ahab has been seen to typify the American spirit.[27] Although Ahab's heroic aura is at time glorified, he maintains the traditional position of the tragic hero by defying the fate that has maimed him—but as Melville's novel demonstrates, larger-than-life actions can exact a high price.[28]

And what is the meaning of this white whale they are pursuing? In Chapter 42, Ishmael's meditates on the whiteness of the whale and the struggle to define the fearfulness of the absence of color in a living thing.[29] This theme of the whiteness of the whale continues throughout the novel; the enigmatic whiteness of the whale seems intertwined with the problem of determining meaning, not only of the whale itself, but of this experience in general.

The connection between Ishmael and Queequeg is extended to an exploration of the interconnectedness of all humanity in Chapter 72, "The Monkey Rope." Ishmael describes being yoked to Queequeg by a rope while Queequeg tries to harpoon a whale and Ishmael, aboard the *Pequod*, struggles to keep Queequeg out of harm's way. Ishmael refers to Queequeg as his twin, and then comments that as human beings, we are all in a similar position, yoked together and relying on each other:

> It was a humorously perilous business for both of us. For, before we proceed further, it must be said that the monkey-rope was fast at both ends; fast to Queequeg's broad canvas belt, and fast to my narrow leather one. So that for better or for worse, we two, for the time, were wedded; and should poor Queequeg sink to rise no more, then both usage and honor demanded, that instead of cutting the cord, it should drag me down in his wake. So, then, an elongated Siamese ligature united us. Queequeg was my own inseparable twin brother; nor could I any way get rid of the dangerous liabilities which the hempen bond entailed.
>
> So strongly and metaphysically did I conceive of my situation then, that while earnestly watching his motions, I seemed to perceive that my own individuality was now merged in a joint stock company of two: that my free will had received a mortal wound; and that another's mistake or

misfortune might plunge innocent me into unmerited disaster and death. Therefore, I saw that here was a sort of interregnum in Providence: for its even-handed equity never could have sanctioned so gross an injustice. And yet still further pondering—while I jerked him now and then from between the whale and the ship, which would threaten to jam him—still further pondering, I say, I saw that this situation of mine was the precise situation of every mortal that breathes; only, in most cases, he, one way or other, has this Siamese connexion with a plurality of other mortals. If your banker breaks, you snap; if your apothecary by mistake sends you poison in your pills, you die. True, you may say that, by exceeding caution, you may possibly escape these and the multitudinous other evil chances of life. But handle Queequeg's monkey-rope heedfully as I would, sometimes he jerked it so, that I came very near sliding overboard. Nor could I possibly forget that, do what I would, I only had the management of one end of it. (p. 256)

The closeness between Ishmael and Queequeg, established earlier in the Spouter Inn and the Counter Pane, is highlighted again in this chapter.[30] Again, the vocabulary of love and marriage is used to describe their relationship, and although we are to take their close relationship literally, perhaps it is also a metaphor for the relations between civilized and "uncivilized," Christian and pagan, western and non-western. These apparently antagonistic groups may in fact have a genuine affinity for one another and their fortunes may rise and fall together, as their fates are truly and inextricably connected. In some ways, this also mirrors Ahab's relationship to his ship and crew. In a larger sense, this passage serves as a reflection on free will, responsibility, and human interconnectedness.

Chapter 110, "Queequeg in his Coffin," presents a minor twist of the plot which later becomes crucial. Queequeg becomes ill and, believing himself near death, asks to have a coffin made such as those he has seen in Nantucket; the coffins remind him of the canoes his people are put into when they die. Queequeg recovers from his illness, but keeps the coffin that the ship's carpenter has made, and carves hieroglyphics into it. (Is he telling his own story as well?) At the end of the novel, Queequeg's coffin serves as the canoe that saves Ishmael's life, so in a sense, in the end, Ishmael is saved by Queequeg, and to some extent, by Queequeg's traditional beliefs. This apparent tangent becomes crucial to Ishmael's survival, and to the narrative itself, because Ishmael is the only surviving witness of the *Pequod*.

Ahab's defiant stance toward the universe and his most strongly held religious beliefs are glimpsed in Chapter 119 "The Candles." Sailing in the direction Ahab has set to pursue Moby-Dick, the *Pequod* is headed toward a typhoon. Starbuck, still reluctant, tells Stubbs that they should turn around and go towards Nantucket. Later, during the storm, they are surrounded by lightning, and the masts resemble candles as they light up with natural electricity. Ahab takes hold of the chain that is supposed to be a lightening rod, and puts his foot on his servant Fedallah, a Parsee, Zorastrian fire worshipper. Captain Ahab utters a prayer that expresses his religion, and says that the proper form of prayer is defiance, an idea consistent with the romantic sensibility. The apparent effect of Ahab's prayer on his men is to engender fear.[31]

We witness Ahab's last opportunity to turn around, head for home, and escape his fate in Chapter 132 "The Symphony," the last chapter before the chase. On this mild, "steel-blue" day, Ahab leans against the ship's railing, looks into the sea and feeling nostalgic, thinks about home. Ahab talks to Starbuck about the deprivations of his forty years at sea, and saying that in his fifties, he has married a girl-bride and is making a widow of her. Starbuck mentions his own wife too, and suggests that they turn around, go back to Nantucket, and forget about Moby-Dick. But just when Starbuck (as well as the reader) thinks that Ahab has been convinced to call off the hunt for Moby-Dick, Ahab starts to talk about destiny again. Like Hamlet, Ahab believes he has a fate to fulfill: "'What is it, what nameless, inscrutable, unearthly thing is it; what cozening hidden lord and master, and cruel, remorseless emperor commands me; that against all natural lovings and longings, I so keep pushing, and crowding, and jamming myself on all the time; recklessly making me ready to do what in my own proper, natural heart I durst not so much as dare?'" (p. 406). When Ahab is finished, he addresses Starbuck, not realizing that he has left in despair. Starbuck's best and last attempt to dissuade Ahab has failed. The fate of Ahab, the *Pequod*, and its crew, have been sealed.

The novel's climax, the physical encounter with Moby-Dick, begins in Chapter 133: "The Chase—First Day." Ahab is the first to spot Moby-Dick; in fact, he literally smells him (p. 407). The reader, along with Ishmael, gets the first view of Moby-Dick. The whale's history is written all over him, because Moby-Dick carries the marks of every wound, and even has harpoons in his hide. The end of the novel is prefigured when, during a chase in a small boat, Ahab falls in the water (p. 410) and is pulled out, physically exhausted.

Ahab's physical pursuit of Moby-Dick continues in Chapter 134: "The Chase—Second Day," with events that are even more foreboding; Fedallah disappears at sea, and Ahab loses his whale-bone leg to Moby-Dick, echoing the loss of his flesh and blood leg, leaving readers to imagine the original trauma. This second loss is almost comical in comparison, but serves as a reminder that this whale can snap through bone, and remove a real limb as easily as an artificial one. Ahab, leaning on Starbuck, says it is "sweet to lean sometimes" (p. 417). Starbuck still feels affection for Ahab but can't seem to stop him, even when Ahab is down to one leg. Here again, one wonders about the inability of Starbuck, Stubbs, and the others to stop Ahab, especially in this chapter in which Ahab is at their mercy, at least in physical terms. If they possessed just a fraction of the defiance that Ahab demonstrates, perhaps they could have averted disaster. Instead of asking the ship's carpenter to make Ahab a new leg, why don't his mates seize control of the ship and go back to Nantucket? Sometimes a little defiance has its value. (Perhaps their reluctance reflects the power of the captain and the hidden dangers of the Mutiny laws, critiqued in *Billy Budd*.) But the opportunity is lost, the ship's carpenter makes Ahab another leg, and the chase resumes, putting the *Pequod* back on course to destruction.

The action continues in Chapter 135: "The Chase—Third Day," as Ahab says goodbye to Starbuck (p. 420). As Moby-Dick appears, the body of Fedallah the Parsee is seen, lashed to the whale by his harpoon rope, an ominous sign of what can happen to he who pursues Leviathan. Ahab has taken Fedallah's place and will serve as harpooner himself. While Ahab acts as harpooner and chases Moby-Dick, the crisis comes as the *Pequod* sinks, broken into pieces by the whale.

As Ahab goes down, he realizes that the strange enigmatic prophesies that he has received, reminiscent of Macbeth, are being fulfilled. For example, Ahab had been told that he need fear only hemp, and as he is dying, he realizes that he is being choked by a hemp rope. In a sense, the whale doesn't destroy Ahab, and Ahab doesn't destroy the whale. Ahab destroys himself, as he is strangled by his own harpoon line and towed under by Moby-Dick.

The entire novel has lead up to this intense but relatively short physical confrontation with Moby-Dick contained in the three brief chapters of the chase. The ending is very compact, perhaps because the key conflicts in the novel aren't physical, and the physical confrontation itself can't be spread over the whole of the novel. But every other kind of conflict is already over, and nothing can persuade Ahab to give up his quest for revenge.

Each day of the chase, Moby-Dick seems more dangerous than the last (providing ample warning for *Pequod* crew) and each day's events more strongly prefigure the disastrous ending. Each day, Ahab comes closer to getting killed: on the first day, he lands in the water and narrowly avoids Moby-Dick's jaws; on the second day, he loses his artificial leg to the whale, and Fedallah disappears into the water; on the third day, the harpoon line wraps around Ahab's neck and pulls him off the boat into water. Once Moby-Dick appears, the *Pequod* meets its end precipitously, and it is all over, except for the Epilogue, and the telling of the tale.

The action slows down in the Epilogue: Ishmael alone survives, "floating on the margin of the ensuing scene" and is being slowly drawn into the (calming) whirlpool when Queequeg's coffin pops up out of the whirlpool. Ishmael climbs into it and spends a day and a night in it, until he is picked up by the ship *Rachel* "that in her retracing search after her missing children, only found another orphan" (p. 427). Again, this final reference to the Bible at the end of the novel is intriguing. The Ishmael of the Bible was the son of Abraham and Haggar; Ishmael and Haggar were cast out by Sarah when she found out she was going to bear Abraham a child, his son, Isaac. In the Bible, Rachel is the wife of Jacob, Isaac's son. Does Ishmael's rescue here by the *Rachel* suggest that Ishmael has been cast out, but is now redeemed?

Ishmael survives to tell the tale, and as the only survivor, he struggles to understand Ahab, not only during the voyage, but afterwards as he recounts the tale as the narrator of *Moby-Dick*. The struggle between Ahab and Moby-Dick has ended; Ishmael's struggle to find meaning in the experience is just beginning.

MEANING IN *MOBY-DICK*

When at the end of *Moby-Dick*, the whirlpool pulls everything into itself, it not only swallows up the *Pequod*, but in a sense swallows up the story of Ahab and Moby-Dick, were it not for the survival of Ishmael who will become the narrator to tell the story. As the *Pequod* disintegrates, so does the world of the fiction, and is ready to disappear—as all novels do. In some ways, this is similar to the whirlwind that destroys the fictional city of Macondo at the end of *One Hundred Years of Solitude* by Gabriel Garcia Marquez.

Ishmael is left to try to make meaning of all this. The struggle to find and make meaning is a major theme in *Moby-Dick*, and language plays a key role in the novel. That role can be seen in Queequeg's tattooed body, or the marks copied onto his coffin, or even the marks on Moby-Dick which suggests the whale's life story. The theme of language continues as Ishmael struggles to come to terms with what has happened through language, even by such impossible means as compiling and studying endless encyclopedic information about whales and whaling.

So Ishmael will struggle through 135 chapters, over 400 pages, to understand his experience. The Homeric lists and apparently encyclopedic efforts to understand everything about whales and whaling are impulses consistent with a schoolmaster narrator like Ishmael, who is doing research to make himself equal to the task of narration, trying through various kinds of information and writings, to understand the experience he has just had. But this experience cannot be understood through an accumulation of factual information, or even through biblical allusions.

Ishmael, along with the reader, struggles to understand the multiple meanings of the White Whale: unconquerable nature; Leviathan from the book of Job; and the whale prepared by God to swallow Jonah. Among the many interpretations of the whiteness of Moby-Dick, some interpretations connect it to the idea of language, writing, and meaning.[32]

Ishmael looks back on what has happened to tell the story, and as he does so, becomes the narrator of *Moby-Dick*, trying to make sense of a narrative that he lived through.[33] This is very much like the distinction between Dante the author of the *Divine Comedy*, and Dante the character in that poem who finds himself lost in the dark words. Ishmael tries to understand what happened partly because he is the sole survivor, and turns to scholarship to try to understand the experience.[34] In this sense, Ishmael can be seen as the narrator of the entire work of *Moby-Dick*, struggling to understand and come to terms with what has happened.[35] It is Ishmael trying to sort out good and evil, Ishmael telling the tale with humor, but also Ishmael looking for meaning by piecing out the most intricate details of whaling, as if that sort of knowledge will help him to understand what really cannot be understood by those means—for Ishmael is not struggling with scientific, historical, or factual questions.

Ishmael and the reader also struggle to understand Ahab. Ahab is a heroic figure who embodies defiance, but at the cost of his ship, his life, and the lives of his crew. Some critics regard him as more mad than defiant[36] and though Ahab sees himself as bound by destiny to his pursuit of Moby-Dick, it is clear finally that Ahab creates the meaning in the event. As has been made apparent in the novel, other responses beyond seeking revenge were available and possible.

If *Moby-Dick* warns of the dangers of a monomaniacal tyrant who defies nature and the universe, it also warns of the dangers of excessive obedience to authority and too little criticism of the charismatic leader. Starbuck is a man sure of his own faith[37] but is nonetheless ineffective in countering Ahab and saving the ship. Could Ahab's destructive mission have gone forward without Starbuck's lackluster do-nothing-ness or without the crew's falling prey to Ahab's charismatic rhetoric? Although the crew knows that their lives are at stake, they do nothing to stop Ahab even when he is down to one leg and is physically at their mercy. However, as we will see, elsewhere in his work, Melville provides models of extraordinary defiance to authority, even in the most ordinary of contexts.

BARTLEBY THE SCRIVENER: A STORY OF WALL STREET

At first, the story of Bartleby the Scrivener seems very different from the rest of Melville's work in both its setting and subject matter, but defiance is not available only to the seafaring adventurer in exotic locations. "Bartleby the Scrivener" presents a character who rejects meaningless work and creates a quiet revolution by passively resisting authority.

The setting is certainly different from what one might expect from Melville or any Romantic writer. Unlike most of Melville's work, the setting of "Bartle by the Scrivener" is mundane rather than exotic and urban rather than natural: a Wall Street with no view of the outside world. But perhaps the point is that a life lived apart from nature, filled only with meaningless work, will produce a Bartleby, who suddenly decides that he prefers not to work, or even eat, or live. The idea that this kind of unnatural and mechanized life destroys the human spirit would certainly be consistent with Romanticism.

Bartleby's actions seem to reflect Emerson's ideas about Transcendentalism that Melville had been reading around the time he composed this tale. "Bartleby the Scrivener" describes no adventure or exciting action, but only a very quiet little revolution that Bartleby carries out by preferring not to (exercising "passive resistance"). In a Wall Street office, he also shows the power of the human spirit to mount a rebellion, however small. This is true even if Bartleby's defiance, like Ahab's, leads to his own destruction.

The story is told by Bartleby's former employer, who hires scriveners to copy papers. He has three employees and decides to hire one more, so Bartleby is hired and installed in his employer's own office. After a short time, Bartleby begins to decline certain tasks saying "I prefer not to," at first politely refusing to proofread for errors, then refusing to do errors, and then finally declines to copy at all. One Sunday, the narrator goes to the office and finds Bartleby there. Bartleby says he is "occupied" and asks his boss to walk around the block first before entering. His employer does so, and soon realizes that Bartleby is living in the office. The narrator is apparently powerless to get this employee to either do his job or move out. Soon, Bartleby takes to simply standing in the office, doing nothing. Finally, his employer moves his business to another location, the only way he can think of to get away from Bartleby. The tenants who move into the old office they find cannot get Bartleby to leave the building, though they have succeeded in keeping him locked out of the office. The new tenants seek out Bartleby's former employer and ask for help. He tries to help, going so far as to invite Bartleby to come live in his house, but Bartleby prefers not to do so. The new tenants have Bartleby taken off to prison, where his former employer visits him. Bartleby now stands around in the courtyard and begins to prefer not to eat, until finally he dies. Afterward the narrator hears rumors that Bartleby used to work in the dead letter office at the Post Office, presumably a depressing and meaningless job.

This story begins with a comic tone, but has a sad ending. The humor comes from the inversions of the roles of employee and employer. Bartleby's quiet refusals quickly invert the social roles of authority of employer and employee. It is surprisingly difficulty for the employer to assert his authority, and it is surprisingly easy for Bartleby to resist. Melville shows us the power of "passive resistance," a phrase that is surprising in "Bartleby the Scrivener," partly because the modern reader associates the term with modern political movements such as the civil rights movements.

The central question is, why does Bartleby prefer not to work? Is he losing interest? Does he find his work meaningless? Critics have raised a variety of explanations as to what it all means.[38] Although some critics explain Bartleby's polite refusal as coming from illness or insanity, it seems more convincing to see Bartleby as a reflection Emerson's philosophy of transcendentalism. Despite speculation that Bartleby is mentally ill, looking at Bartleby's situation, words, and actions, as well as evidence that Melville read Emerson's essay, it seems safe to assume that Bartleby's choices express that philosophy, as some have maintained.[39] Transcendentalists are idealists, not materialists, and what is relevant to "Bartleby the Scrivener" is that transcendentalists are enjoined to reject and avoid any activity they don't think worthy or meaningful, including work. Melville is said to have read Emerson's "Transcendentalist" very carefully as he began "Bartleby;" and the annotated version of Emerson's text in Norton Critical Editions of *Melville's Short Novels* suggests in the footnotes which passages are relevant to Bartleby.[40] The philosophy of transcendentalism is consistent with Romanticism in giving the individual the right to break any rule because of innately divine human nature.[41]

Another controversy around "Bartleby the Scrivener" is the character of the narrator, who is seen as a crass materialist by some, but a better, more sensitive reading is that of Dan McCall ("The Reliable Narrator") who suggests that the older and wiser narrator is aware of his former flaws and is extremely sensitive to Bartleby's situation, possibly because he identifies with the issues.[42]

How does "Bartleby the Scrivener" reflect Melville's American Romanticism? Melville shows the negative power of a life lived without contact with nature, without meaningful work, and without passion. In addition, "Bartleby the Scrivener" shows that defying authority can be accomplished quite effectively (and politely) by an ordinary person. (Could Bartleby have stood up to Ahab?)

BILLY BUDD

Billy Budd, written towards the end of Melville's life and published posthumously, is also a story about authority and freedom. It is Romantic in its portrayal of the unschooled innocent, and in the questions it raises about authority, law, and defiance in society. It is a narrative that seems to suggest multiple meanings.

The beautiful orphaned Billy Budd is a British boy, a valued crew member of a ship called *The Rights of Man*, which is boarded by an officer of a military ship, the *Bellipotent*, to conscript some men, and Billy is the only one chosen. On the new ship, Billy is liked by everyone except James Claggart, master-at-arms, who takes an instant dislike to Billy. Claggart hates Billy for unidentifiable reasons, perhaps jealousy or desire caused by his beauty. Billy is puzzled when he is taken to task for minor infractions and even more puzzled when another sailor approaches him and asks him to join in a mutinous plot. Billy refuses, but does not report the incident, an action which perhaps would have helped him avoid the problems that develop. For unknown reasons, Claggart goes to Captain Vere and falsely accuses Billy of plotting mutiny. Captain Vere calls Billy into his office where Billy has to listen to Claggart's false accusation, but due to a bad stutter that renders him inarticulate under stress, Billy cannot make an answer. Enraged and speechless, he hits Claggart in the head, killing him instantly. Vere asserts that military rules demand that Billy be tried for treason—for striking an officer and killing him—as well as for mutiny, but the only possible witness that the charge was false is the person that Billy has killed.

There is a quick trial, and as Melville says, some thought too quickly (p. 148). Vere is witness, judge, jury, and executioner. So Captain Vere, who on the face of things, seems to be a good man and a sympathetic character, believes himself obligated, even forced, to put Billy to death, the next morning. This takes place in the context of recent mutinies and maintaining order is important. The captain doesn't want to execute Billy, but he will do so. Immediately before dying, Billy blesses Captain Vere.

Billy's death is more peaceful than is usually the case at hangings; he doesn't even twitch. Afterwards, sailors keep pieces of the gallows on which Billy was hanged as if they were pieces of the cross. Eventually Billy becomes a kind of folk hero, and a song is even written about him. There are several references to Christianity and to Billy as a Christ-like figure, and also to the innocent Adam before the Fall. He is called a peacemaker; he is betrayed, and virtue is said to emanate from him as from Jesus of Nazareth.

On the other hand, Vere seems to a good person at heart, but also a remote, disciplinary, and scholarly man. He is certainly not ruled by his heart, though he obviously has one. He prefers to do things by the book. He seems to be divided from his authentic and spontaneous emotions, from his best self, and makes the greatest errors when he elevates rules and hierarchy above his feelings. Immediately after Claggart dies, Vere says, "Struck dead by an angel of God," a spontaneous and accurate assessment, but in the next sentence Vere expresses his decision that that the angel of God must die. Vere even recognizes the difference between the judgment God might make about Billy, and the judgment that he is forced to make as a ship's captain. The notion that emotions should be given more weight than rules is certainly consistent with the Romantic sensibility and Vere squelches his natural emotional impulses and native conscience—impulses that French Romantic philosophers, such as Rousseau, see as innately good.

Thus, a critique of a mindless and unfeeling application of the rules would be consistent with Romanticism. It is interesting that the setting for *Billy Budd* is a British ship, not an American one. Did Melville want to avoid criticizing American military? Melville had himself deserted one ship and been involved in a mutinous situation on another ship.[43] Although it would be difficult to conceive of Melville favoring Vere's decision, he does seem sympathetic towards Vere, and understands that in a way Vere is as much a victim of the rules as Billy.

Although Billy is called a peacemaker by the captain of the *Rights of Man*, in that same breath that same captain describes a situation in which Billy has hit someone. "Quick as lightening Billy let fly his arm." Billy gets tongue-tied under strong emotion, and then lashes out. This not only identifies Billy as a hothead within the first few chapters, but also foreshadows the fatal action that will lead to Billy's trial. He is also described as Adam before the Fall:[44] "... Billy in many respects was little more than a sort of upright barbarian, much such perhaps as Adam presumably might have been ere the urbane Serpent wriggled himself into his company" (110). Thus, Billy's portrayal of an innocent aligns him more with the innocent Adam, complete with all the human impulses, good and bad, than with a Christ-like figure.

On the face of it, the events of the story are horrifying. Captain Vere thinks he is doing the right thing and seems to be caught by circumstance, forced to put Billy to death. However, Melville's narrative seems to lead readers to ask some harder questions about what happens.

Vere is extremely upset, perhaps as Melville suggests, a little bit out of his mind, immediately after Claggart's death. The narrator says that the ship's surgeon was "disturbed by the excited manner he had never before observed in the *Bellipotent's* captain" (146). Why is he so upset? Captain Vere's emotion is obvious. We get to see his emotion. But why is he in such a hurry for the trial, haste which is questioned in the story itself?

Melville's statements about the role of the chaplain in the military can be taken as tantamount to an indictment of the Church.[45] This helps readers to put Vere's actions in perspective, especially when Vere says that God's judgment would acquit Billy, but the military will not. This is a critique of authoritarian systems of rule such as the military and religion. If Vere were willing to listen to his own heart and soul, Billy wouldn't be executed.

Jealousy and passion are proposed as motivations for Claggart, who says he could love Billy if not for fate and bans. Some critics have suggested that that Vere is also attracted to Billy. That Vere notes Billy's attractiveness is borne out by the text.[46] Is Vere going out of his way to be fair, in spite of special feelings, and ending up being so much more than unfair?

Despite the controversy over Captain Vere, several critics have pointed out Vere's lack of basic fairness and inability to uphold the principles of law in his procedures.[47] In fact, *Billy Budd* is used as a text in some law schools.[48] Although Billy likes Captain Vere, Billy is said to be extremely innocent and naive. Billy doesn't blame Vere, but that doesn't mean that the reader should not. A final note casts doubt on Vere's integrity: the newspaper account of the story about Billy is very inaccurate, saying that Billy stabbed Claggert with a knife. It is a final indictment of Vere that he didn't see to it that the story was corrected.

The narrative of *Billy Budd* establishes an imperfect world in which people are cornered, or think they are cornered, into making terrible choices, into doing the wrong thing for the right reasons. It also suggests that the blind application of rules can create terrible injustice and reflects the romantic idea that natural instincts and emotions are better than the rational rules and constraints of government and civilization.

Is *Billy Budd* a critique of the mutiny laws themselves? Melville repeatedly shows the problems that arise when a captain with extremely strong authority somehow goes wrong and becomes fixated on an idea like Captain Ahab, or makes rigid decisions like Captain Vere.

CONCLUSION

Melville's works contain major themes that demonstrate his unique perspective as an American Romantic through his enduring interest in sea voyages, exotic cultures, and indigenous peoples; his recognition of the power of human emotion; and his interest in enduring questions of defiance, authority, and the individual will.

As works of American Romanticism, Melville's writings remain instructive as the modern world struggles with issues of identity and its place in the natural world. It instructs so long as we insist on domination rather than stewardship; so long as we remain ignorant of other languages and cultures at our own peril; and so long as we are creatures of emotion as well as reason.

NOTES

1. Hershel Parker, in "Damned by Dollars: *Moby-Dick* and the Price of Genius" in *Moby-Dick*, Norton Critical Edition (NY: W.W. Norton, 2002). Delivered as a talk at the Old Dartmouth Historical Society New Bedford Whaling Museum at Johnny Cake Hill as the Samuel D. Rusitzky Lecture on June 26, 1997.

2. Joyce Carol Oates, Introduction to *Herman Melville, Billy Budd and Other Tales*, p. xi. Signet Classics (NY: New American Library, 1998). Originally published in *The Ontario Review*, July 1998.

3. In their Preface to the Norton Critical Edition of *Moby-Dick* (New York, W.W. Norton & Co., 2002), Hershel Parker and Harrison Hayford describe Melville as a "slightly belated, and American" Romantic, p. ix.

4. For more on Melville's political ideas, see Carolyn L. Karchner, "Melville and Revolution," in *Melville's Short Novels*, Norton Critical Editions, (NY: W.W. Norton and Co., 2002), p. 344. Originally published in *Shadow over the Promised Land; Slavery, Race and Violence in Melville's America*, (Baton Rouge, LA: Louisiana State University Press, 1980).

5. Harold Bloom, in "Gnosticism: The Religion of Literature," says that this term "was first employed in the seventeenth century to describe the ancient 'heresy' that existed among later first century pagans, Jews and Christians. Nearly all our indisputably Gnostic texts are second-century Christian, but earlier Jewish tradition had worshipped 'the primal Adam' as the authentic prophet." p. xviii, *Genius: A Mosaic of One Hundred Exemplary Creative Minds* (NY: Warner Books, Inc., 2002).

6. See Bloom, "Gnosticism: the Religion of Literature" in *Genius*, p. xviii.

7. See Chronology, p. 239, in *Herman Melville*, Bloom's Modern Critical Views, edited and with an introduction by Harold Bloom (New York: Chelsea House Publishers, 1986).

8. In their Preface to *Moby Dick*, Norton Critical Edition, Parker and Hayford write "Many of the geopolitical themes Melville dealt with from his own experiences—Pacific Rim commerce, colonialism, deliberate or careless destruction of indigenous cultures and environments, exploitation of nature, racism, enslavement, immigration—are themes uppermost in the minds of many modern Americans" (p. x).

9. As Parker & Hayford point out in their Preface to the Norton Critical Edition of *Moby-Dick*, Melville was "thinking globally" at the same time that "many Americans were using the Monroe Doctrine to justify isolationism" (p. ix).

10. This may also explain some of the doubling of characters and loose ends that Harrison Hayford discusses in "Unnecessary Duplicates: A Key to the Writing of *Moby-Dick*," in the Norton Critical Edition of *Moby-Dick*, published in 2002, originally published in *New Perspectives on Melville*, edited by Faith Pullen (Edinburgh: Edinburgh University Press, 1978) pp. 128–61. See also Parker's essay "Damned by Dollars: Moby-Dick and the Price of Genius" for a discussion of the constraints and rapidity of Melville's composition due to his financial situation.

11. For example, Bulkington was not written out of the novel once Queequeg was added. See Hayford, "Unnecessary Duplicates: A Key to the Writing of *Moby-Dick*."

12. Walter E. Bezanson, in "Moby-Dick: Work of Art" points out that "To go from *The Scarlet Letter* to *Moby-Dick* is to move from the Newtonian world-as-machine to the Darwinian world-as-organism. In the older cosmology the key concepts had been law, balance, harmony, reason; in the newer, they became origin, process, development, growth. Concurrently biological images arose to take the place of the older mechanical analogies: growing plants and life forms now symbolized cosmic ultimates better than a watch or the slow-turning rods and gears of an eighteenth-century orrery" (p. 655). *Moby-Dick*, Norton Critical Editions, 2002. Previously published in *Moby-Dick: Centennial Essays*, edited by Tyrus Hillway and Lurther S. Mansfield (Dallas: Southern Methodist University Press, 1943).

13. Parker in "Damned by Dollars: Moby-Dick and the Price of Genius," p. 714 of *Moby-Dick*, Norton Critical Editions, 2002.

14. In "The Early Novels," Newton Arvin says that *Typee* and *Omoo*: "... tell the story of a quest or pilgrimage ... from the world of enlightened rationality, technical progress, and cultural complexity backward and downward and, so to say, inward to the primordial world that *was* before metals, before the alphabet, before cities; the slower, graver, nakeder world of stone, of carved wood, of the tribe, of the ritual dance and human sacrifice and the prerational myth" (p. 41). "The Early Novels: *Typee, Omoo, Redburn, White-Jacket*," in *Herman Melville*, Bloom's Modern Critical Views, edited and with an introduction by Harold Bloom (New York: Chelsea House Publishers, 1986). Originally

published in *Herman Melville* (William Sloane Associates: Greenwood Press, Inc., 1950).

15. Bezanson, in *"Moby-Dick*: Work of Art," points out that in the seventeenth century, "discovering the use of whale products especially the oil for lighting, man begins to bring to bear on the pursuit of whales the technologies developed in transportation and war" and that in the nineteenth century, "the United States ... builds a whaling fleet of over seven hundred vessels and commits itself to a sea frontier that girdles the globe. New Bedford, Nantucket, and Sag Harbor become the world centers for the pursuit of sperm whales" (p. 642).

16. Bezanson says, in *"Moby-Dick*: Work of Art," that *Moby-Dick* is about "not Indian fighting or railroad building but whaling" (p. 641).

17. See Hayword, "Unnecessary Duplicates: A Key to the Writing of *Moby-Dick*."

18. Bloom calls Ahab an "American King Lear" in his essay "Herman Melville", in "Lustre 8: Nathaniel Hawthorne, Herman Melville, Charlotte Bronte, Emily Jane Bronte, Virginia Woolfe," *Genius* (p. 308). Joyce Carol Oates, in her introduction to Melville's *Billy Budd* (p. ix), calls Melville's "tragic vision as elevated as that of Sophocles and Shakespeare."

19. Bloom says that "... Ishmael and Queequeg were involved in the covenant with Ahab, to hunt down and slay the great white Leviathan, exalted by God in the Book of Job as the authorized tyranny of nature over man." *Genius* (p. 299).

20. Bloom says that Ahab expresses an "American defiance" when he vows that "I'd strike the sun if it insulted me", *Genius* (p. 306).

21. Bloom points out that nearly none of the characters on the *Pequod* are Christian and that Ahab is Gnostic. Bloom writes: "It should be recalled always that the *Pequod*, despite Quaker ownership, has a mostly Pagan crew. Starbuck may be the only Christian on board; Fedallah and his group are Parsee Zoroastrians. Ishmael is a Neoplatonist, Stubbs and Flask are atheists, and there are a dozen or more animist faiths scattered among the others." "Herman Melville," *Genius* (p. 308).

22. Bloom writes, "Ahab is not a Christian, and like William Blake, he believes that the god of this world, called by the names of Jesus and Jehovah, is a botching demiurge, who has set Moby-Dick to reign over us in the same way that Jehovah sends Leviathan and Behemoth against poor Job." "Herman Melville," *Genius* (p. 307).

23. Bloom says that Ahab is Gnostic, converted from Zoroastroaism, *Genius* (p. 307).

24. See Bloom's excellent analysis of this passage in *Genius* (p. 31–312).

25. Hayden's "Unnecessary Duplicates: a Key to the Writing of *Moby-Dick*" discusses characters that are not written out of the novel when they are replaced by new characters. Hayden's believes *Moby-Dick* was written in stages and that as Melville came up with a new character, he didn't completely discard the old. (Parker's essay "Damned by Dollars: Moby-Dick and the Price of Genius" illuminates the financial pressures for rapid production which might not have allowed Melville sufficient time to revise.)

26. See also Bezanson, *"Moby-Dick*: Work of Art."

27. Bloom calls Ahab "the American Prometheus," *Genius* (p. 307).

28. Bloom objects to moralizing scholars who make Ahab a villain. Bloom says, "Ahab is no villain, not even a hero-villain like Macbeth. More than our sympathies are with Ahab: we are Ahab. He tasks us, he heaps us, for he is the hero as American, our tragic Don Quixote, questing for ultimate justice over the last enemy, death," *Genius* (p. 306).

29. For more on the phenomenology of whiteness in *Moby-Dick*, see Paul Brodtkorb Jr., *Ishmael's White World: A Phenomenological Reading of 'Moby Dick'* (New Haven, CT: Yale University Press, 1965).

30. Camille Paglia says, "*Moby-Dick* begins with a ritual of male bonding. Ishmael and Queequeg are tied by 'matrimonial' language and bedroom embraces." (*"Moby-Dick* as Sexual Protest" in *Moby-Dick*, Norton Critical Editions, 2002, p. 700). Originally published in *Sexual Personae: Art and Decadence from Nefertiti to Emily Dickinson* (New Haven, CT: Yale University Press, 1990).

31. In his introduction to *Herman Melville*, Bloom writes: "If Ahab has a religion, it is Persian or rather Parsee, and so Zoroastrian. But Melville has not written a Zoroastrian hymn to the benign light for Ahab to chant. Ahab's invocation is clearly Gnostic in spirit and in substance, since the light is hailed as being both ambiguous and ambivalent." *Herman Melville*, Bloom's Modern Critical Views (p. 7).

32. Paglia says that *Moby-Dick* "takes the whiteness or blankness of nonmeaning as its premier symbol" [*"Moby-Dick* as Sexual Protest"] (p. 697).

33. Bezanson points out that there are two Ishmaels, Ishmael the narrator and the young Ishmael who goes to sea. "The first Ishmael is the enfolding sensibility of the novel, the hand that writes the tale, the imagination through which all matters of the book pass. He is the

narrator.... The second Ishmael is not the narrator, not the informing presence, but is the young man of whom, among others, narrator Ishmael tells us in his story. He is simply one of the characters in the novel, though to be sure a major one whose significance is possibly next to Ahab's. This is forecastle Ishmael or the younger Ishmael of 'some years ago'" "*Moby-Dick*: Work of Art" (p. 644).

34. Bezanson says the narrator has undertaken these studies to try to understand his experience, and is "sifting memory and imagination in search of the many meanings of the dark adventure he has experienced" "*Moby-Dick*: Work of Art" (p. 645). "So deeply are we under the spell of the narrator's voice that when at last the final incantation begins—'And I only am escaped alone to tell thee'.... The drama's done.... —then at last, as forecastle Ishmael floats out of the *Pequod's* vortex, saved, we look again on the face of Ishmael narrator. And we realize that for many hours he has been sitting there and has never once moved, except at the lips; sitting in profound reverie, yet talking, trying to explain 'in some dim, random way' what happened, for 'explain myself I must.'" "*Moby-Dick*: Work of Art" (p. 645).

35. Harrison Hayford, in "'Loomings': Yarns and Figures in the Fabric" says of the narrator: "My critical strategy is to take the narrative, from its opening sentence 'Call me Ishmael,' as altogether the work of Ishmael, its ostensible narrator, and to interpret all its elements as coming from Ishmael and hence characterizing Ishmael, not Melville. In this way the dense imaginative coherence is transferred from the book and its author to the mind of Ishmael as its ground and cause. In this perspective, the action of the work takes place in the observing and participating mind of Ishmael. His mind 'contains' the tragedy of Ahab as Ishmael confronted it some years ago in experience and now confronts it once again in the telling" in *Moby-Dick*, Norton Critical Editions, 2002 (p. 657). Originally published in *Artful Thunder: Versions of the Romantic Tradition in Honor of Howard P. Vincent*, edited by Robert J. deMott and Sanford E. Marovitz (Kent, OH: Kent State University Press, 1975).

36. John Wenke, for example, in "Ahab and the 'Larger, Darker, Deeper Part," talks of Ahab's madness and even mentions a "schizoid split," (p. 703). *Moby-Dick*, Norton Critical Editions. Reprinted from John Wenke, *Melville's Muse: Literary Creation and the Forms of Philosophical Fiction* (Kent, OH: Kent State University Press, 1995).

37. Bezanson says that Starbuck "... stands alone in his sturdy, limited world of facts and settled faith." "*Moby-Dick*: Work of Art" (p. 651).

38. Oates sees Bartleby as a "precursor of the cipher-figures of Kafka, Beckett, Ionesco..." and asks, "... Is he, perhaps, an alter ego of the narrator's, as of Melville himself, refusing to participate in the fixed, dull, routine, if inevitable, rituals of a money-making society in which all are 'copyists' and originality is discouraged" (p. ix), "Introduction" to *Herman Melville: Billy Budd and Other Tales*.

39. See Ralph Waldo Emerson's "The Transcendentalist" in *Melville's Short Novels*, edited by Dan McCall (Norton Critical Editions, NY: W.W. Norton, 2002). Also, Bloom points out that "... both attracted and repelled by Emerson, Melville haunted Emerson's lectures and scribbled fierce marginalia in Emerson's essays." In "Herman Melville," *Genius* (p. 307).

40. "The Transcendentalist adopts the whole connection of spiritual doctrine. He believes in miracle, in the perpetual openness of the human mind to new influx of light and power; he believes in inspiration, and in ecstasy." Emerson, "The Transcendentalist," *Melville's Short Novels*, Norton Critical Editions (p. 188). Reprint of a lecture read at the Masonic Temple, Boston, January 1842.

41. See p. 189 of "The Transcendentalist." The following paragraph is noted by the editors of *Melville's Short Novels*, Norton Critical Editions to be "a likely source for the figure of Bartleby" (footnote 3, p. 190): "It is a sign of our times, conspicuous to the coarsest observer, that many intelligent and religious persons withdraw themselves from the common labors and competitions of the market and the caucus, and betake themselves to a certain solitary and critical way of living from which no solid fruit has yet appeared to justify their separation. They hold themselves aloof; they feel the disproportion between their faculties and the work offered them, and they prefer to ramble in the country and perish of ennui, to the degradation of such charities and such ambitions as the city can propose to them. They are striking work, and crying out for something worthy to do" (p. 190). Also, "They prolong their privilege of childhood in this wise, of doing nothing,—but making immense demands on all the gladiators of wealth and fame" (p. 192).

42. Dan McCall, "The Reliable Narrator" in *Melville's Short Novels*, edited by Dan McCall, (W.W. Norton, 2002).

43. See p. 680 of *The Cambridge History of American Literature*.

44. This passage illustrates what Bloom says about Adam, that before the Fall he had perfect innocence, and was closer to the divine because he was made directly by God.

45. Robert K. Martin Jr.'s in "Is Vere a Hero?" says "The Church has been turned into an arm of the state and hence becomes a collaborator in murder (the execution of prisoners) and war. Over and over again Melville has called attention to the role of the military chaplain, who by accepting that post betrays the Church to which he claims allegiance.... The chaplain on the *Bellipotent* is 'the minister of Christ though receiving his stipend from Mars.'" *Melville's Short Novels*, Norton Critical Editions, (NY: W.W. Norton, 2002) p. 364.

46. Mervyn Cooke, "Homosexuality in *Billy Budd*" suggests that both Vere and Claggart are attracted to him, and gives a pretty compelling quotation from Vere about the beauty of Billy Budd: "The veiled allusions to shipboard homosexuality in the novella (no doubt still derived from Melville's earlier first-hand observations of sexual behaviour at sea) form an undeniably important element of the story. Homosexual lust is a chief foundation for Claggart's hatred of Billy, and even Vere's attitude towards the foretopman is more than altruistically paternal ("he had congratulated Lieutenant Ratcliffe upon his good fortune in lighting on such a fine specimen of the *genus homo*, who in the nude might have posed for a statue of the young Adam before the Fall"). Claggart's sexual attraction for Billy reaches a climax in every sense in the incident described at length in Chapters 10 and 13, when Billy spills his bowl of soup at Claggart's feet...." (p. 359). From *Melville's Short Novels*, Norton Critical Editions. Originally published in Mervyn Cooke and Philip Reed, *Benjamin Britton, Billy Budd* (NY: Cambridge University Press, 1993).

47. Hershel Parker in "From the Plot of Billy Budd and the Politics of Interpreting it" (p. 341), points out that people's opinions about Vere are determined by their politics, but that on (p. 341) that "In rapid sequence the captain leads (or coerces) a hastily convened court martial to conclude what he wants it to conclude" (p. 341). From "The Plot of Billy Budd and the Politics of Interpreting It" in *Herman Melville's Short Novels*, Norton Critical Editions. Reprinted from Hershel Parker, *Reading Billy Budd* (Evanston, IL: Northwestern University Press, 1990). The article by Robert K. Martin, "[Is Vere a Hero?]" shows Melville's indictment of Vere, coming through Vere's own words; see pp. 363–364. Martin points out that Vere's actions don't hold up as a man of law: "... he betrays the very code he claims to believe in. It is not even necessary to accept the idea of a moral code higher than military justice (although I am certain that Melville did so) in order to condemn Vere.

Revolution may be a legitimate fear, but does it justify the suspension of legal procedure? And if Vere acts only out of a justified fear of mutiny, why not act on that basis instead of cloaking his behavior in legal self-righteousness? Surely the first obligation of a court is to determine evidence; that this court never does. Vere is the accuser, the witness, and the judge; he is even the defense counsel at moments. No witnesses are heard; no attempt is ever made to determine the truth of Claggart's accusation ..." *Melville's Short Novels*, Norton Critical Editions (p. 362) Martin also says that Vere's actions don't hold up legally, because he is witness, judge and executioner. "Nothing that we know about the role of the Captain from the earlier works would lead us to believe that Melville would create a captain who represents the moral perspective of the author: every Captain in Melville is corrupt, a tyrant, or a madman. But it is of course possible that Melville came to reject everything he had once believed. Let us look then more carefully at Melville's characterization of Vere" (p. 362). Martin's analysis goes on to show Vere to be a snob, a tyrant, and less than great as a man of law. See pp. 362–363.

48. Tom Goldstein, in "Once Again, Billy Budd Is Standing Trial," discusses legal opinions about Billy Budd. In *Melville's Short Novels*, Norton Critical Editions. Originally published in the *New York Times*, June 19, 1988.

Works Cited

Arvin, Newton. "The Early Novels: 'Typee,' 'Omoo,' 'Redburn,' 'White-Jacket'", *Herman Melville*. William Sloan Associates Inc., Greenwood Press Inc., 1950.

Bezanson, Walter E. "*Moby-Dick:* Work of Art," in Norton Critical Editions; previously published in *Moby-Dick: Centennial Essays*, edited by Tyrus Hillway and Lurhter S. Mansfield (Dallas: Southern Methodist University Press, 1943).

Bloom, Harold. "Herman Melville" in "Lustre 8: Nathaniel Hawthorne, Herman Melville, Charlotte Bronte, Emily Jane Bronte, Virginia Woolf" in *Genius: A Mosaic of One Hundred Exemplary Creative Minds*. NY: Warner Books, Inc.; 2002.

Brodtkorb, Paul Jr. "Ishmael's White World: A Phenomenological Reading of '*Moby Dick.*'" New Haven, CT: Yale University Press, 1965.

Cooke, Mervyn. "Homosexuality in *Billy Budd*." From Mervyn Cooke and Philip Reed, *Benjamin Britten, Billy Budd*. New York: Cambridge University Press, 1993.

Emerson, Ralph Waldo. *The Transcendentalist*. In *Melville's Short Novels*, Norton Critical Edition. (NY: W.W. Norton, 2002). Reprint of a lecture read at the Masonic Temple, Boston, January, 1842.

Goldstein, Tom. "Once Again, 'Billy Budd' Is Standing Trial," in Norton Critical Editions; Originally published in the *New York Times*, June 19, 1988.

Hayford, Harrison. "Loomings: Yarns and Figures in the Fabric" in Norton Critical Editions; originally published in *Artful Thunder: Versions of the Romantic tradition in Honor of Howard P. Vincent*. Edited by Robert J. deMott and Sanford E. Marovitz. Kent, OH: Kent State University Press, 1975.

Hayford, Harrison. "Unnecessary Duplicates: A Key to the Writing of *Moby-Dick*," in Norton Critical Editions. Originally published in *New Perspectives on Melville*. Edited by Faith Pullen. Edinburgh: Edinburgh University Press, 1978.

Hayford, Harrison and Hershel Parker, "Preface," *Moby-Dick*, Norton Critical Editions. NY: W.W. Norton, 2002.

Karchner, Carolyn L. "Melville and Revolution." *Melville's Short Novels*. Norton Critical Editions. NY: W.W. Norton, 2002, p. 344. Originally published in *Shadow Over the Promised Land; Slavery, Race and Violence in Melville's America*. Baton Rouge, LA: Louisiana State University Press, 1980.

Martin, Robert K. Jr. "Is Vere a Hero?" from *Hero, Captain, and Stranger: Male Friendship, Social Critique, and Literary Form in the Sea Novels of Herman Melville*. University of North Carolina Press, 1986.

McCall, Dan. From "The Reliable Narrator," *Melville's Short Novels*. Norton Critical Editions. NY: W.W. Norton, 2002. Reprinted from Dan McCall, *The Silence of Bartleby*. Ithaca, NY: Cornell University Press, 1989.

Oates, Joyce Carol. "Introduction." *Herman Melville's Billy Budd and Other Tales*. Signet Classics, 1998. NY: New American Library. The introduction first appeared in *The Ontario Review*, July 1998.

Paglia, Camille, "*Moby-Dick* as Sexual Protest" in *Moby-Dick*, Norton Critical Editions. From *Sexual Personae: Art and Decadence from Nefertiti to Emily Dickinson*. New Haven, CT: Yale University Press, 1990.

Parker, Hershel. "Damned by Dollars: *Moby-Dick* and the Price of Genius" in *Moby-Dick*. Norton Critical Edition (NY: W.W. Norton, 2002). Originally delivered as a talk at the Old Dartmouth Historical Society New Bedford Whaling Museum at Johnny Cake Hill as the Samuel D. Rusitzky Lecture on June 26, 1997.

Parker, Hershel. "From the Plot of *Billy Budd* and the Politics of Interpreting it." *Herman Melville's Short Novels*, Norton Critical Editions. Reprinted from Hershel Parker, *Reading Billy Budd.* Evanston, IL: Northwestern University Press, 1990.

Wenke, John. "Ahab and the 'Larger, Darker, Deeper Part," Norton Critical Editions p. 702–711. Reprinted from John Wenke, *Melville's Muse: Literary Creation and the Forms of Philosophical Fiction.* Kent, OH: Kent State University Press, 1995.

NEWTON ARVIN

The Author of Typee, Omoo, &c.

Most modern writers have come to the literary career in response to a
vocation of which they have been conscious from boyhood on; if they
have not lisped in numbers, they have at any rate filled their adolescence
with plans for novels, for ambitious poems, for plays. One cannot say
flatly that this was not true of Melville; we do not know whether it was
or not. But in spite of the "Fragments from a Writing-Desk," one's
impression is that Melville came to literature, not after long and
conscious preparation, but with a kind of inadvertence. He speaks of
having dreamed as a boy of becoming a great traveler and even of
becoming a famous orator but never of becoming an author. The need
for movement, for flight, for the coarse stuff of experience was stronger
in him in his earliest youth than the need for expression. The germ of
what was creative in him needed to ripen, not in solitude or in
intellectual labor, but in the push and stir of action. In the beginning, for
Melville, was decidedly not the word, but the deed. Not until he had to
come to terms with the dense material world and the actualities of the
human struggle was he prepared to give himself out in language and
form. His development, in that sense, as he recognized, had been
abnormally postponed, and when it came, it came with a rush and a force
that had the menace of quick exhaustion in it. Could it possibly be
maintained at that pitch over the span of a long career?

From *Herman Melville* by Newton Arvin. © 1950 by William Sloane Associates, Inc.
Renewed 1978 by the children of author Newton Arvin. Reprinted by permission of
HarperCollins Publishers.

That remained to be seen, but meanwhile, in just this respect, in the postponement of creation to action, Melville makes one think, not of the representative modern man of letters, for whom action has been either secondary or without significance, but of a heterogeneous list of writers, as different from one another as from him in power and in character, writers like Smollett or Stendhal or Fenimore Cooper or Tolstoy, who spent their earliest years, not at their writing desks, but on the deck of a ship or in the train of a marching army. Bookish as Melville had always been and was increasingly to be, he came to the profession of letters as a kind of brilliant amateur, and he was never quite to take on, whether for better or for worse, the mentality of the professional.

This is hardly to say that he was a lesser writer than those who did. Nor certainly is it to say, on a more superficial level, that he was not, once he had found his tongue, almost unaccountably productive. One imagines him writing *Typee* in much the same spirit in which Dana had written *Two Years* or in which the young Englishman Kinglake was writing *Eothen*: because he had seen a bit of the world, because his head was stored with fresh impressions and entertaining circumstances, and because his relatives and friends had drawn him out in conversation in a way that aroused and ignited him. No doubt he wrote *Typee* almost casually; it turned into a great success before his eyes; his powerful literary instincts were fully awakened, and there followed, during the next five or six years, at a breathless pace, four other books—*Omoo, Mardi, Redburn,* and *White-Jacket*—in the composition of which he can hardly have paused or deliberated. Neither Dana nor Kinglake had done anything of the sort, and that is one difference between them and Melville.

This was the school of writing, nevertheless, that furnished Melville his springboard as an artist. It was no mere accident that it did so, but a characteristic fact that holds for no other nineteenth-century writer of his stature. He did not begin at once, like most of them, as a writer of tales, sketches, or novels for the periodicals or the booksellers' libraries of the era; he did not begin as a successor of Sterne or Godwin or Scott, of Mrs. Radcliffe or Hoffmann. He began as one more writer of travel narrative, and the books from which he took off were not *Tristram Shandy* or *Waverly* but Mungo Park's *Travels in the Interior of Africa*, the Rev. C.S. Stewart's *Visit to the South Seas*, and of course the book he called "my friend Dana's unmatchable *Two Years Before the Mast*." Saying this is something like saying that George Eliot began as a writer of critical and philosophical articles for the *Westminster Review*; no other writer of just that sort has gone on to write books like *Middlemarch*, and none of the other writers of "travels" or "journals" or "narratives" went on to write books like *Moby Dick*. But George Eliot's whole work is pervaded by the attitudes of the moralist and critic, and Melville, for his part, was always to be an imaginative writer for whom the facts of movement through space, of change of site, of physical unrestingness and the forward push were basic. The voyage or quest was not simply a subject or an occasion for him; it was an archetypal pattern of experience to which his whole nature instinctively turned, and he was to lose half his strength not when he lost contact with the earth but when he stood still upon it.

Typee and *Omoo*, to be sure, were books that he wrote, if not off the top of his mind, at any rate off its less profound levels, and it is idle to look for great depths or difficulties in them; to do so would be to miss their special quality of spontaneity and youthfulness. Yet there are intimations of complexity in them, and in a purely literary sense, easy though they seem, they are curiously many-faceted. They owe something, in a general way, to the whole tradition of travel literature since the modern age of discovery began, and particularly to the voyages of the eighteenth century, to the writers of the age of Cook and Carteret and Bougainville, whose aim was always to be lucid, impersonal, informative; to suppress *themselves* and to convey the facts, however novel or strange, with the most reasonable and enlightened objectivity. A love of information for its own sake was one of the aspects of Melville's complex mind, as every reader of *Moby Dick* knows; and when, in *Typee*, he describes the process of making tapa or the operations of the system of tabu, or when, in *Omoo*, he dilates on the botany and the economy of the coco-palm, his tone and manner are not easily distinguishable from those in which Captain Cook or Bougainville or Langsdorff had expatiated on exactly similar subjects. Melville's first two books have been quoted by anthropologists since his time, by Sir James Frazer for example, as having at least some claim to trustworthiness, despite Melville's very small comprehension of the language of Taipi or Tahiti. The fact is that, whenever his imagination was at work most freely and naturally, it sought for and found the factual, prosaic counterpoise to the inwardness and ideality that were its essential expression; and *Typee* and *Omoo* owe much of their vitality to their apparently unpoetic ballast of facts.

A transformation, however, had taken place in the literature of travel since the eighteenth century, just as it had done in literature generally, and such books could no longer be written sustainedly in the old manner, any more than novels could be written in the manner of Diderot or Smollett. The dry, clear, sober impersonality of the older writers had given place to a more and more frankly personal and subjective style, whimsical, humorous, lyrical, sentimental, or poetic; Melville began writing in a period that had formed its taste on such lighthearted and charming books as Heine's *Pictures of Travel*, Irving's *Alhambra*, Kinglake's *Eothen*, and Gautier's *Travels in Spain*. Information of a kind does indeed appear in books like these, but what really counts in them is not that but feeling, fancy, atmosphere, and the effort to evoke as many and as brilliant pictures as possible. The sense of the painterly has usurped the place of the older interest in fact.

Even in a writer like Mungo Park, at the turn of the nineteenth century, one detects already a strain of personal feeling and even a sense of the pictorial that is by no means merely "eighteenth century"; and Mungo Park was almost certainly one of Melville's literary masters. There are deeply moving passages in Park's *Travels*, but what happened to travel writing after his time becomes evident when one turns to Melville abruptly from a writer of his sort. Here is a passage, quite typical of Park's ordinary narrative style, from his account of a night spent at an African town in the kingdom of Kajaaga:

> I found a great crowd surrounding a party who were dancing by the light of some large fires, to the music of four drums, which were beat with great exactness and uniformity. The dances, however, consisted more in wanton gestures than in muscular exertion or graceful attitudes. The ladies vied with each other in displaying the most voluptuous movements imaginable.

Compare with this—in its quiet, taciturn failure to realize a potentially quite wonderful picture—compare with it Melville's description in *Omoo* of the dancing girls at Tamai or, better yet, this description in *Typee* of a fishing party returning from the beach at night:

> Once, I remember, the party arrived at midnight; but the unseasonableness of the hour did not repress the impatience

of the islanders. The carriers dispatched from the Ti were to be seen hurrying in all directions through the deep groves; each individual preceded by a boy bearing a flaming torch of dried cocoa-nut boughs, which from time to time was replenished from the materials scattered along the path. The wild glare of these enormous flambeaux, lighting up with a startling brilliancy the innermost recesses of the vale, and seen moving rapidly along beneath the canopy of leaves, the savage shout of the excited messengers sounding the news of their approach, which was answered on all sides, and the strange appearances [...] seen against the gloomy background, produced altogether an effect upon my mind that I shall long remember.

Naturally this is not yet Melville in his great evocative vein, and Stevenson was later to outdo him, just here, in finish and precision of brush stroke, but the passage will serve as a fair example of Melville's painterliness in *Typee* and *Omoo.* Like some other passages in those books, it hints to us—with its romantic chiaroscuro, its violent contrast of deep shadow and high flaring lights, the uncanniness of its moving figures, and its dependence on words like "wild," "startling," "strange," and "gloomy"—hints to us that Melville, in looking at the scenes that passed before him and in reinvoking them, had learned something from such Gothic writers as Mrs. Radcliffe and "Monk" Lewis, and that through them, perhaps also independently, his landscape sense had been formed by the Baroque painters they were always echoing, by Claude Lorrain and Salvator Rosa. Salvator in the Marquesas might have done the nocturne of the fishing party. Baroque, at any rate, most of Melville's landscapes and seascapes certainly are, as well as many of the other scenes he composes like pictures. The hours he spent as a boy poring over the portfolios of prints Allan Melville had brought home had worked a permanent influence on his imagination.

His first two books abound in pictorial effects that can only be described as in some sense romantic; wild and fearful like the gorges, ravines, and chasms of Nuku-Hiva through which he and Toby make their painful way in *Typee*; solemn, deeply shaded, and awe-inspiring, like the tabu groves in Taipi-Vai; uncannily beautiful like another fishing party by torchlight, in *Omoo,* in the sullen surf off Moorea; or in a wholly different vein—the vein of Claude rather than of Salvator—pastoral,

Arcadian, richly reposeful, like the first breathless glimpse of the Paradisal valley of Taipi. Already in these early, experimental books, with varying degrees of success, Melville knows how to cover a gamut of painterly and emotional effects that ranges all the way from the broad and serene to the wild, the grim, and even the grotesque. And indeed it is evident that these contrasts of tone and feeling, especially marked in *Typee*, are conscious and artful, not merely inadvertent, and that they express a native feeling for structure and style that already suggests how much farther Melville may go as an imaginative writer than any of the narrators he is emulating. *Two Years Before the Mast* is a greater book than either *Typee* or *Omoo*, in its strong, sustained austerity of style as well as in its grandeur of feeling; but Melville's books are the unmistakable products of a far more complex and ductile mind than Dana's, and potentially, of course, of a richer creative power. Dana's great book suggests no artistic mode beyond itself; *Typee* and *Omoo* hint constantly at the freer and more plastic form of fiction.

When they first appeared, indeed, they were taxed, or credited, by many readers with being *pure* fiction, and some of these readers, at least, were more imaginative than those who took them for sober fact. It is not only that we now know how long a bow Melville was drawing in both books, especially *Typee*; how freely he was improvising on the mere actualities of his experience; that is an external and mechanical sort of check. The books themselves need only to be read responsively in order to uncover their real quality—their real and equivocal quality of narrative that is constantly vibrating between the poles of "truthfulness" and fantasy. The proportion of sober truthfulness in *Omoo* is doubtless greater than in *Typee*, and the free, fanciful strains in it take the form of playfulness, gay exaggeration, and grotesqueness rather than, as they mostly do in *Typee*, of a heightened "anxiety," on the one hand, and a deliberate idyllism, on the other. But in both books Melville is far too much the born artist not to keep bathing the plain truth in a medium of imaginative intensity.

A few weeks after *Typee* was published, as we have seen, Toby Greene unexpectedly turned up in Buffalo to testify to the veracity of those chapters for which he could vouch, but we must not take his evidence too literally. Melville's story of what happened after he and Toby plunged into the interior of Nuku-Hiva, of the hardships and sufferings they underwent before they arrived in Taipi—this story bears on the face of it the hallmarks of poetic sublimation. Plenty of travelers have undergone greater ordeals than Melville's was at its worst, and one has only, again, to read Mungo Park's account of some of his solitary vicissitudes in order to observe how calmly and even barely the thing can be done. There is nothing calm or bare and certainly nothing austere in Melville's narrative. It is frankly and volubly a tale of tribulation: it abounds in the imagery of physical and mental misery. At the outset Melville and Toby are drenched by a downpour of tropical rain; they find themselves trapped in a thicket of dense, resistant reeds; they are baked by the heat of midday; they scramble up a steep cliff and crawl along a ridge on their bellies to evade detection; they are confronted by a series of "dark and fearful chasms, separated by sharp-crested and perpendicular ridges," up and down which they painfully clamber; they spend the nights in gloomy ravines, shivering with the chill and dampness; and at last they make their way down into the valley by falling, rather than descending, from ledge to ledge of a horridly high, steep precipice. Throughout, they suffer from hunger and raging thirst; Melville, from a painful injury to his leg; and both of them, from "frightful anticipations of evil." We move, in all this, not over the solid terrain of even a romantic island but amidst a dream-imagery of deadly apprehensiveness, baffled and dismayed by obstacle after obstacle, and oppressed continually by a dread of what is before us. Such writing is far less reminiscent of *Two Years* than it is of Mrs. Radcliffe or Poe.

The note of nightmarish foreboding, in any case, is struck recurrently in *Typee*, where it reaches a culmination of intensity in the last chapters, with Melville's gruesome discoveries and his horror lest he should be powerless to escape. It alternates, however, like a theme in music, with the strongly contrasted note of contentment and peace; the contentment and peace of daydreaming. The conflict between wishful revery and the anxiety that springs from a feeling of guilt, in short, goes on throughout the book. In *Omoo*, on the other hand, perhaps because it was written in a period of emotional freedom and effervescence, there is no such inner drama and no such stylistic musicality. The contrasts of tone in the book are furnished partly by the simple alternation between personal narrative and impersonal informativeness, but also by the relatively prosaic setting-off of the hardships and exasperations of life aboard the *Julia* (Melville's name for the *Lucy Ann*) or in the Calabooza Beretanee against the heady pleasures of freedom and vagrancy. The play of fantasy in *Omoo* takes the form not of nightmarishness or even of daydreaming but of an easy and emotionally liberating current of humorous narrative, always slightly in excess, as one sees with half an eye, of the sober autobiographical facts. It usually has the satisfactory effect of throwing a ludicrous light on the representatives of order and authority—captains and mates, consuls and missionaries, resident physicians and native constables. There is still, as a result, an emotional release in reading *Omoo*, as in reading any such book; we take our own revenge on respectability by contemplating the discomfiture of the feeble Captain Guy and the bullying consul Wilson, or by listening to the wily sermon of the Chadband whom Melville describes himself as hearing in the church at Papeete.

It is true that, compared with the billows of almost demoniac humor on which *Moby Dick* is so incredibly sustained, the humor of *Typee* and even of *Omoo* seems gentle and rather tame. Yet one feels at once that it is the expression of a genuinely humorous fancy. One feels it in such accounts as that of the popgun war in *Typee* or of Long Ghost's jolly philanderings in *Omoo*. One feels it even verbally in such remarks as that Captain Guy was "no more meant for the sea than a hairdresser," or in the observation on the ugliness of the ship's carpenter on the *Julia*: "There was no absolute deformity about the man; he was symmetrically ugly." One feels this youthful humor chiefly, however, in the individual characters in whom both books abound, and who are treated with a freedom far closer to fiction than to mere reminiscence. The difference is easily evident when one puts one of Dana's characters—say the young Hawaiian, Hope, or the English sailor, George P. Marsh, a decayed gentleman—side by side with characters like Melville's Kory-Kory or Long Ghost. Dana's portraits have the sobriety and the realism of Copley's in another medium; Melville's come closer to suggesting Cruikshank or Phiz. For the rest, in the period when he was writing *Typee* and *Omoo*, it was mostly the amusing, even lovable oddities and humors of human character that engaged him, not its darknesses and depravities. There are shadows of some intensity here and there; in the brutal Captain Vangs and in the dark, moody, vindictive Maori harpooneer, Bembo; but mostly the scene is animated by such gently comic personages as fussy old Marheyo in Taipi, or the grotesque-looking Kory-Kory, or the poor landlubber sailor, Ropey, on the *Julia*.

Most of them are mere sketches, lightly and hastily drawn; and the most fully realized feminine character, the exquisite Fayaway, is not so much drawn as vaguely and dreamily evoked in wishful water colors. Only one personage among them all is painted at full length; this is the

demoted ship's surgeon, Long Ghost, who is the real protagonist of
Omoo (Melville himself is the protagonist of *Typee*), and who embodies
the complete footlooseness, the perfect irresponsibility, which Melville,
on one side of his nature, would have liked to attain. A ruined
gentleman, well-read and well-mannered, but lazy, mischievous,
reckless, amorous, and rascally, Long Ghost appears in the forecastle of
the *Julia* as if he were a personal materialization of all Melville's longings
for a really unbraced and ungirded freedom. So long as the mood lasts,
Long Ghost sticks by his side, a perfect companion, indeed another self;
but at length the mood passes, the fundamental seriousness in Melville
reasserts itself, and about to join the crew of the *Leviathan* he takes leave
both of the waggish doctor and, to all intents and purposes, of the
beachcomber in himself.

The gesture has an almost allegorical quality. Lighthearted and
unprofound as on the whole they are, *Typee* and *Omoo* have an undertone
of serious meaning. Taken together they tell the story of a quest or
pilgrimage—a pilgrimage not, certainly, "from this world to that which
is to come," but from the world of enlightened rationality, technical
progress, and cultural complexity backward and downward and, so to
say, inward to the primordial world that *was* before metals, before the
alphabet, before cities; the slower, graver, nakeder world of stone, of
carved wood, of the tribe, of the ritual dance and human sacrifice and
the prerational myth. It was a pilgrimage that led to no all-answering
oracle or consummatory revelation; in that sense it was a failure. But it
was a pilgrimage that Melville's deepest needs had driven him to make,
and he did not return from it empty-handed. There are passages in *Typee*
especially that tell us how really intense, how far from merely
fashionable, was his animus against "civilized barbarity," against "the
tainted atmosphere of a feverish civilization." He returned to civilization
in the end, but he had had a long gaze at a simpler, freer, gayer, and yet
also statelier mode of life, and this was to serve him, in memory, as a
stabilizing and fortifying image. His own creative power, moreover, at its
height, was primeval and myth-making in a sense that, in his day, was of
the rarest: it could never have been set free, just as it was, if he himself
had not made his descent into the canyon of the past. In touching the
body of Fayaway, Melville had regained contact with the almost
vanished life of myth.

His instincts had guided him rightly when they sent him
wandering into the young Pacific world, and they guided him rightly

when they drove him away from it again and back to civilized society, to resume a burden he had temporarily laid down—the burden of consciousness, of the full and anguished consciousness of modern man. He had taken a long plunge into the realm of the preconscious and the instinctual, the realm of heedless impulse and irreflective drift; he had been refreshed, indeed remade, by it; but he had found there no ultimate resolution of his difficulties. Not in avoiding the clash between consciousness and the unconscious, between mind and emotion, between anxious doubt and confident belief, but in confronting these antinomies head-on and, hopefully, transcending them—in that direction, as Melville intuitively saw, lay his right future as an adult person. The alternative was a lifetime of raffish vagrancy with the seedy Long Ghost, and a kind of Conradian dilapidation at the end. In the last chapter of *Omoo*, saying good-bye to his companion, he insists on Long Ghost's taking half the Spanish dollars which the captain of the *Leviathan* has given him as an advance; a generous but also a proper payment for the wisdom he has acquired in Long Ghost's society. A new cruise awaits him, on another vessel; and in fact, when Melville finished the writing of *Omoo*, he had come to the end of one expedition, in the intellectual and literary sense, and was ready to set out again in a quite different direction.

The writing of *Typee* and *Omoo*, it goes without saying, confronted Melville with literary problems, but they were not problems of intense difficulty, and in solving them he was content for the most part to rely on a literary form that was already fully evolved and perfectly well defined when he began to write. He could do this because what he was aiming to express was an experience, or rather an aspect of that experience, that was relatively unprofound, uncomplex, unproblematic. Other writers of such books had stopped dead in their tracks at just that point, but naturally this was impossible for Melville. Only now, as he later remarked to Hawthorne, was he beginning to be aware of an intense inward development, of an almost painfully accelerated process of unfolding within himself; only now, in his middle and later twenties, was he becoming fully conscious of a thousand intellectual and emotional perplexities, difficulties, enigmas. Month by month, one imagines, as he was writing *Typee* and surely *Omoo*, the need was growing on him to descend deeper and deeper into these obscure and questionable regions of the mind, and to move on, as a writer, from the manner of an American Gautier or Kinglake to a larger, bolder, more complex, and more symbolic manner that would be capable of rendering the richness and the fullness of his maturing thought.

There was little in the literary practice of Melville's generation to make this process of discovery anything but a troubled and wasteful one. The romantic tale, as Hoffmann and Poe had developed it, was too purely static and introverted, as well as too confined, ever to have been a natural form for Melville to turn to at this stage; and he could not move, as Hawthorne had done, from the romantic tale to the psychological romance, from "Young Goodman Brown" to *The Scarlet Letter*. The great form of the historical novel had already passed its meridian, and even if it had not, it was only too evidently unprofitable to Melville, for whom the past did not have the emotional and poetic value it had for Scott and Hugo. "The Past is the text-book of tyrants," he says in *White-Jacket*; and though the remark naturally does not exhaust the range of Melville's feelings about history, it helps one to understand his development as an artist. Still less than in the historical romance, moreover, could he find his account in the practice of his great contemporaries, Balzac and Stendhal, Dickens and Thackeray: his imagination shared no common ground with these observers of the social, the contemporary scene, of business, the church, the great world, the modern city. His solution did not lie in the main direction of the nineteenth-century novel.

What he did, as a result, when he came to write *Mardi*, was to grope his way forward toward a new manner by writing alternately in several manners, no one of them quite the right one. The book begins in very much the vein of *Typee* and *Omoo*, though the air of the fictional is now still more pronounced, and when Melville and his elderly companion Jarl desert the *Arcturion* and set off in a whaleboat, one soon finds oneself in the nautical novelistic world of Cooper and Marryat, of *Wing-and-Wing* and *Mr. Midshipman Easy*. Then abruptly, and quite without transition, appears the great double canoe of Aleema and his sons, with the fair Yillah as a prisoner in it, and one steps suddenly into the region of romantic or transcendental allegory, of *Heinrich von Öfterdingen* and the Blue Flower, or of Huldbrand von Ringstetten and the water-sprite, Undine. More or less at the same time one enters a far less worthy, far weedier literary region than that, but a related one: the region of sentimental symbolism and gift-book prettiness, of "the language of flowers," of the *Atlantic Souvenir* and *Godey's Lady's Book*.

Something in Melville responded to the mincing *marivaudage* of conversation at Miss Anne Lynch's, where he sometimes turned up at this period; and just as Poe could make common cause with Mrs. Seba Smith, or Whitman with Fanny Fern, so Melville, with the amaranths and oleanders which Hautia's messengers keep brandishing before Taji, joins hands with Mrs. Fanny Osgood and *The Poetry of Flowers*.

Aleema, Yillah, and Hautia, however, and the romantic-sentimental allegory they embody, make their presence felt only at intervals in the later chapters of *Mardi*. When Yillah mysteriously vanishes, one turns with Melville—or Taji, as he is now called—to the company of the cheerful South Sea king and demigod, Media, and sets out with him and other companions on a voyage round the archipelago of Mardi—in quest, to be sure, of the unforgotten Yillah but also for the sake of visiting one quite independently allegorical island after another. Much of what follows is in the ancient line of philosophical and ethical satire; in the line, not of Novalis and de la Motte Fouqué, and certainly not of Mrs. Osgood, but of Lucian, Rabelais, and Swift. On the whole, this was a somewhat less infelicitous vein for Melville, somewhat less of a pitfall for him, than the other.

Taji's voyage, in any case, reminds one at once of Lucian's fantastic trip beyond the Gates of Hercules in the *True History*, or of Pantagruel's quest for the Oracle of the Holy Bottle, or of Gulliver's voyages to Lilliput and Brobdingnag. When Taji, Media, and the others sail past what Melville calls Nora-Bamma, the Isle of Nods, one thinks of Lucian and his visit to the slumbrous Isle of Dreams. The whole voyage from island to island is full of reminiscences of Rabelais, especially of his last two books. The praise of eating and drinking is highly Rabelaisian in intention, and so in general is all the satire on bigotry, dogmatism, and pedantry. Taji and his friends wandering about on the island of Maramma, which stands for ecclesiastical tyranny and dogmatism, are bound to recall Pantagruel and his companions wandering among the superstitious inhabitants of Papimany; and the pedantic, pseudo-philosophical jargon of Melville's Doxodox is surely, for a reader of Rabelais, an echo of the style of Master Janotus de Bragmardo holding forth polysyllabically to Gargantua in Book I. As for *Gulliver's Travels*, there is something very Swiftian in Melville's Hooloomooloo, the Isle of Cripples, the inhabitants of which are all twisted and deformed, and whose shapeless king is horrified at the straight, strong figures of his visitors from over sea. Hooloomooloo is but one of several reminders of

Swift, and in general, though all this was nowhere near the center of Melville's imagination, it was in a vein that was far more natural to him than that of romantic allegory: some of these Rabelaisian or Swiftian passages—that on the same Isle of Cripples, as an instance—are done with a certain vivacity and point.

There are suggestions of other familiar literary modes in *Mardi*, but from this point of view the most remarkable thing about the book is Melville's attempt to endue it with the enchantment of the exotic and also with the grandeur of the legendary and mythical by using, throughout, the imagery of Polynesian life. It was an effort that deserved to succeed better than it did: Melville, after all, was the first Western writer of genius who had lived in the South Seas himself, and he was the first of the actual travelers to go beyond mere narrative and to aim at converting his remembered impressions into serious, ambitious, and poetic fiction. So the seascape and landscape of Mardi is that of the Pacific world, of Hawaii or the Marquesas or Tahiti: a chain of high-peaked islands, set in their rings of coral reefs and lagoons, abounding in seaside groves and inland valleys, shaded by the foliage of breadfruit and casuarina trees, of coco-palms and hibiscus, and dotted here and there with the thatched and open dwellings of the natives. These dwellings are furnished with mats and tapa hangings, with gourds and calabashes; the feasts that are consumed in them consist of breadfruit dishes, baked yams, and tropical fruits; and the feasters are clothed in tapa tunics and mantles, in garlands and wreaths; the more aristocratic of them, in feathered ornaments that are purely Hawaiian. The sacred edifices, moreover, are not temples but *morais*, like the great Morai of Maramma, which allegorically suggests St. Peter's at Rome but pictorially resembles some great Polynesian *morai* like that of Purea on Tahiti.

Nor is the Polynesianism of *Mardi* a matter only of scene: it is a matter also of custom and conduct, of legend and myth. It is true that Melville was drawing, in all this, not only on his own memory but also on the reading he had done both earlier and later, and that many a passage in *Mardi* derives, in the literal sense, rather from William Ellis's *Polynesian Researches* than from Melville's days in Taipi or Maatea. But in the deeper sense it was those days, those recollected impressions, that made *Mardi* possible: Ellis and the others were only tools for the forming imagination—tools, to be sure, that were not always handled with perfect skill. In any case, the South Sea localism of manners and

behavior is inescapable in *Mardi*. The girdle of Teei, which is the symbol
of kingship on the Isle of Juam, might have been the *maro-ura* or girdle
of red feathers that, according to Henry Adams, was the symbol of
chiefship in old Tahiti; and when the common people in Mardi strip to
the waist in honor of their chiefs, they are only observing a form of
obeisance that in fact prevailed in the South Seas. There chiefs were
actually, as they are in Mardi, regarded as gods or demigods, and when
the narrator of the novel represents himself as being taken for the
returned god Taji, Melville is of course remembering how Captain Cook
was taken by the Hawaiians for the returned god Lono. When Mohi,
Melville's chronicler, relates the early history of Juam and the struggles
between Teei and his brother Marjora, one might be listening to some
narrative of the violent career of an actual Pomare or Kamehameha.
Indeed the precipice of Mondo in *Mardi*, over the brink of which, says
Melville, fifty rebel warriors were driven to their deaths, can hardly fail
to suggest the real cliff called the Nuuanu Pali, on the Hawaiian island
of Oahu, over the brink of which the first Kamehameha did actually
drive his worsted enemies.

Beyond all this, however, Melville was feeling his way forward,
rather timidly and fumblingly, to a genuinely mythopoeic form by
investing his narrative with something of the quality of Polynesian
legend and myth. The attempt was on the whole an abortive one, but the
important thing is that he made it. The whole tale of the priest Aleema
and his lovely captive Yillah suggests an awkward mingling of something
that might be a Tahitian or Hawaiian legend with something that might
be a German romantic allegory. Yillah herself suggests, on the one hand,
some particularly vaporous Mathilda or Undine and, on the other, some
legendary Hawaiian maiden, a Kaanaelike or Kamamalau, of whom
Melville might conceivably have heard. As the voyagers sail past the
islanded crag of Pella, Mohi the chronicler tells a story to account for its
being there, and this story recalls a local legend about a mountain near
Papetoai on Moorea, which Melville himself had of course seen. On one
island or another Taji hears of the names and deeds of various gods,
Keevi the god of thieves, for example, or the nimble god Roo. Somehow
these unvenerable deities strongly suggest certain real Polynesian
gods—or better, perhaps, such a tricky culture-hero as the great Maui,
the Polynesian Prometheus, who fished up the various islands of the
Pacific with his magic fish-hook. Mardi, at all events, abounds in gods as
Polynesia did, and the name of the great transcendent god of Mardi,

Oro, was in fact the name of a real deity in Tahiti. Yet it must be confessed that, in all this, *Mardi* remains a sketch, a promise, an intimation, and not a consummated achievement.

It does so partly because, in spite of Taipi and Fayaway, the specific myths and legends of Polynesia remained somewhere near the surface of Melville's mind and imagination; their special quality of feeling and image-making somehow kept them from serving as the vehicles of his deepest experiences; it was only as legend and myth in general that they attracted and liberated him. His own myth-making, when its time came, was to be the expression of his own culture and his own age and not, predictably, that of the neolithic world of the Pacific islands. Moreover, the thoughts and feelings he was attempting to express in *Mardi* were too disparate among themselves and often too incongruous with his South Sea imagery to be capable of fusion into a satisfying artistic whole. In the rush and press of creative excitement that swept upon him in these months, Melville was trying to compose three or four books simultaneously: he failed, in the strict sense, to compose even one.

Mardi has several centers, and the result is not a balanced design. There is an emotional center, an intellectual center, a social and political center; and though they are by no means utterly unrelated to one another, they do not occupy the same point in space. The emotional center of the book is the relation between Taji and Yillah, between the "I" and the mysterious blonde maiden he rescues from the priest Aleema, at the cost of slaying him; the maiden with whom he dwells for a short time in perfect felicity on a little islet off the coast of Odo, but who then vanishes as mysteriously as she has appeared. Taji sets out in quest of her throughout Mardi; he fails to find her on one island after another; he fails, in the end, to find her at all, but he discovers that she has fallen a victim to the witchcraft of the enchantress Hautia, and in ultimate despair, convinced that life without Yillah would be "a fife of dying," he turns his prow at last toward the open sea of self-destruction.

In the poetic sense the whole allegory of Yillah is too tenuous and too pretty to be anything but an artistic miscarriage. In the personal and biographical sense, and in connection with the rest of Melville's work, it is extremely revealing. The blonde and bloodless Yillah, who in the language of flowers is associated with the lily, is an embodiment of the pure, innocent, essentially sexless happiness which, given his relations with his mother, Melville longed to find in his relations with some other woman, and which he had some reason to feel he had at one time fleetingly enjoyed. Even then—we do not know why—he had enjoyed it only at the expense of some act of emotional violence, of injury to another; and such happiness as he had had was soon destroyed by the intrusion of the sensual, the carnal, the engrossingly sexual, of which Hautia, symbolized by the dahlia, is the embodiment. With all of this the most intense and anguished emotions of remorse are associated: they drove Melville, in *Mardi*, to an act of symbolic suicide. It is possible that he was expressing thus the emotional history of his marriage to Elizabeth Shaw, which took place during the summer of 1847, perhaps after he had written the first, seagoing chapters of *Mardi*, but certainly before he had written the greater part of the book. It may be that the abrupt break at the end of the thirty-eighth chapter occurred at the time of the wedding and honeymoon, and in any case the allegory of Yillah and Hautia is strongly suggestive of the passage from an idealized courtship to the fleshly realities of marriage. What is not open to doubt is that physical sexuality was charged through and through for Melville with guilt and anxiety.

Meanwhile the middle portion of *Mardi* is mainly occupied by a series of forays in social and political satire, and by quasi-metaphysical speculations, that are at the best only loosely and uncertainly related to the quest for Yillah: the attempt to weave them together into a unified fabric was almost as quixotic as the attempt would be to find a common frame for *Endymion* and *A Connecticut Yankee*. If the fabric of *Mardi* holds together at all, it is only because there is a certain congruity among the various more or less frustrated quests it dramatizes—the quest for an emotional security once possessed, the quest for a just and happy sociality once too easily assumed possible, and the quest for an absolute and transcendent Truth once imagined to exist and still longed for.

The social and political strictures which are so explicitly expressed in *Mardi* are sometimes astonishingly sweeping and severe: they force us to remember that, though the deep centers of his work lie elsewhere, Melville was all along, among other things, a writer of the critical and protestant order to which Carlyle, Thoreau, and Tolstoy belonged. Partly under the sway of writers like this, no doubt, but much more under the bombardment of his own harshly instructive experience— "bowed to the brunt of things," as he says, "before my prime"—Melville had conceived an attitude toward the civilization of his age that mingled in quite special and personal fusion the ingredients of skepticism, humorous contempt, and the anger of an outraged sense of right. It is not great passion, for example, but it is a real enough disdain that inspires his treatment of the fashionable world in *Mardi*—in the allegory of the silly Tapparians and their insipid, formalized life on the island of Pimminee. There is a much deeper note in the satire on militarism as one sees it in the sanguinary war games constantly being played on the Isle of Diranda. There is a deeper note still in the glimpse one has, behind the charming fore-scene on Odo, of the broken serfs and helots who labor in the *taro* trenches and dwell in noisome caves; of the horrors of industrialism on the island of Dominora, which is the England of Dickens and Engels; and of the collared people, toiling under the eyes of armed overseers, in the extreme south even of republican Vivenza.

Vivenza is of course Melville's own country, and *Mardi* expresses, with no attempt at a forced consistency, both the pride he always felt in being an American—"in that land seems more of good than elsewhere"—and the skeptical reservations with which he contemplated America's present and future. It is not that these reservations leave one in any uncertainty where Melville's feelings as a democratic writer lay: the indictment of arbitrary political power and an inhumane or rigidified inequality is unambiguous enough. What he rejects is not the profounder moralities of democracy—they were in his blood—but a cluster of delusions and inessentials that, as he felt, had got themselves entangled with the idea of democracy in American minds; the delusion that political and social freedom is an ultimate good, however empty of content; that equality should be a literal fact as well as a spiritual ideal; that physical and moral evil are rapidly receding before the footsteps of Progress. All this Melville rejects, and he counters it with a group of insights that are by no means always sharp and strong; they are sometimes feeble and sometimes capricious; but in their wiser expressions they take the form of a political and social pessimism that was for him wholly reconcilable with a democratic humanism, though certainly not with an optimistic one. "For evil is the chronic malady of the universe."

So reads, in part, a scroll which the travelers find fixed against a palm tree in Vivenza: it is Melville's somber retort not only to the overweening political hopefulness of his time and place but to its optimistic ethics and metaphysics as well; to the unmodulated affirmations to which Emerson had given the most exaggerated expression: "Through the years and the centuries ... a great and beneficent tendency irresistibly streams." Melville saw no such tendency in nature or in history; on the contrary, he had failed to find in nature any warrant for the aspirations of humanity ("nature is not for us") and he had failed to find in history—or in his own experience—any warrant for a belief in human perfectibility. Man he had very generally found to be a "pugnacious animal," "but one member of a fighting world," and his discovery had not filled him with confidence in the human outlook. On the whole, experience and reflection had confirmed the dark view of the natural man which his Calvinist nurture had implanted in him. They had not, however, confirmed the metaphysical absolutes of Calvinism, or indeed absolutes of any sort; and the philosophical plot of *Mardi* is furnished by the interaction—which, to tell the truth, is too largely a vacillation—between the longing for certainty, a longing at least as intense as that for Yillah, and the painfully recurring suspicion that, on all the great questions, "final, last thoughts you mortals have none; nor can have."

"Faith is to the thoughtless, doubts to the thinker," says one of Melville's spokesmen in *Mardi*, and in the end Taji himself cannot find spiritual assurance even in the pristine, purified, undogmatic Christianity of Serenia. Meanwhile, however, it is clear that Melville is struggling to avoid "a brutality of indiscriminate skepticism," as he calls it, and no doubt—divided and confused as he was, when he wrote the book, among a host of contradictory emotions and ideas—he came nearest to expressing his basic thought in a speech of Babbalanja's as he "discourses in the dark": "Be it enough for us to know that Oro"—God—"indubitably is. My lord! my lord! sick with the spectacle of the madness of men, and broken with spontaneous doubts, I sometimes see but two things in all Mardi to believe:—that I myself exist, and that I can most happily, or least miserably exist, by the practice of righteousness."

It is not a very trumpet-tongued conclusion, nor even philosophically a very remarkable one, and indispensable though *Mardi* is to a study of Melville's developing powers—fine, even, as a few passages in it are—the book suffers irremediably, as a work of art, from the intellectual precipitateness and prematurity out of the midst of which it was palpably written. If Melville could have brought himself, at that period, to confide his crowding thoughts to the pages of a personal journal, the result might well have been a gradual burning up of his own smoke and, in the end, the pure lucidity of tragic insight that is consistent with dramatic and poetic wholeness. As it is, what one mostly finds in *Mardi* is not the clarifying solemnity of tragic acceptance; it is the drifting and eddying fog of intellectual worry, vacillation, and indecision, and in consequence there is no imaginative purification in reading it. Doubt and repudiation are great themes, and great books have been written on them; mere indecisiveness is strictly speaking not a theme for a work of art at all, and despite the violent termination of *Mardi*, its general movement is that of indecision rather than of strong denial.

This is what essentially keeps the personages, the narrative, and the symbols themselves from really enlisting our imaginative interest and taking a sure hold on our imaginative attention; most readers will end by agreeing with T.E. Lawrence that *Mardi*, as a whole, is a dull book. A remark of Eliot's may also occur to some of them: "We cannot afford to forget that the first—and not one of the least difficult—requirements of either prose or verse is that it should be interesting." Melville was quite capable of remembering just this, and doubtless it is with a momentary flash of self-criticism that he remarks in *Mardi* itself: "Genius is full of trash." If *Mardi* is a mixture of trash and genuineness, however, it is the sort of mixture of which only genius is capable. The unalloyed metal still remained to be run into the molds.

In both the intellectual and the literary senses *Mardi* had turned out, despite its undeniable qualities, to be a great detour for Melville; in the end it brought him back to his own route but in an oblique and rather wasteful way. His mind was still developing too rapidly and too intensely for him to be long content with the kind of skepticism, impatient and even intemperate, which *Mardi* ended by expressing. There is a lesser skepticism and a larger one, and the skepticism of this book is not yet the latter. In its form and texture, too, *Mardi* was evidently not what Melville was struggling to arrive at; he made no second use of its characteristic manner, and years later he was to voice his true feeling about the book when he remarked that the worst thing he could say about Richter's *Titan* was that "it is a little better than *Mardi*." His central problem as a writer was to find a fictional style in which there would be a particular kind of dynamic balance between fact and form, between concept and symbol, between the general and the particular—"the whole problem is there," as Gide once observed—and Melville had by no means found his solution in transcendental allegory of the Early Romantic type or even in the ancient mode of satirical burlesque he had inherited from Rabelais and Swift. Just how flimsy

Yillah and Hautia are as vehicles for Melville's meaning is evident when one reflects for a moment on the essential unnaturalness and unspontaneity, for him, of the flower images that accompany them, the un-Melvillean verbenas and vervain; and as for the Rabelaisian tour of the archipelago of Mardi, it grows more and more perfunctory and essayistic as the book wears on.

Manqué though it was, however, *Mardi* had been written, we may be sure, at the cost of a heavy drain on Melville's psychological resources, and he was not yet ready to move on to another effort of comparable scope and difficulty: time would have to elapse before his highest energies could accumulate their full weight and force. Meanwhile it was a question of lowering his sights a degree or two, and what he did when he went on to write *Redburn* and *White-Jacket* had superficially the air of a return upon himself, a lapse back to the vein he had already worked in *Typee* and *Omoo*, the vein not of metaphysical allegory but of unpretentious reminiscent narrative, vibrating again between the poles of literal autobiography and free fictional improvisation. *Redburn* and *White-Jacket* take us back once more to the ship and the sea voyage, to "real" ships and "real" seas: in the one case, to the deck of an American merchant vessel making an ordinary trip across the North Atlantic; in the other, to the deck of an American man-of-war on its cruise from the port of Callao in Peru, around the Horn, back to its home port on the eastern seaboard. Both books abound in information, in factuality, in solid objects and practical activities, and in all this they recall *Typee* and *Omoo*. But the movement Melville was describing, it need hardly be said, was not a retrograde but a spiral one, and *Redburn* and *White-Jacket*, though they have lost the youthful charm of the earlier books, are denser in substance, richer in feeling, tauter, more complex, more connotative in texture and imagery. Whatever imperfections they may have, they give us the clear sense that the man who wrote them was again on his own track.

The prose, for one thing, is that of a much more mature person and more expert writer. One easily sees how much ground Melville has gained, partly as a result of writing *Mardi*, when one turns from almost any page of the first two books to almost any page of the later ones. Here is a characteristic passage from *Omoo*:

> Toward morning, finding the heat of the forecastle unpleasant, I ascended to the deck, where everything was

noiseless. The Trades were blowing with a mild, steady strain upon the canvas, and the ship heading right out into the immense blank of the Western Pacific. The watch were asleep. With one foot resting on the rudder, even the man at the helm nodded, and the mate himself, with arms folded, was leaning against the capstan.

On such a night, and all alone, revery was inevitable. I leaned over the side, and could not help thinking of the strange objects we might be sailing over.

Certainly the nocturnal picture here is pleasantly rendered; the effect of contrasted motion and stillness (the advancing ship, the nodding helmsman, and the like) is quickly and agreeably achieved; the rhythms are easy; the forward movement of the sentences is steady and effortless; the plain, low-pitched diction surges a little, at one moment, to a kind of grandeur in the phrase, "the immense blank of the Western Pacific." But rhythmically the passage achieves little more than easiness; the language is almost neutral and without idiosyncrasy; and the sense of a missed opportunity in the last sentence is acute. There are finer passages in *Typee* and *Omoo*, but virtually nowhere in those books does Melville write as he repeatedly writes in *Redburn* or *White-Jacket*. Is it possible, in such a passage as the following, from *Redburn*, to mistake the gain in rhythmical variety and intricacy, in sharpness of diction, in syntactical resource, in painterly bravura and the fusing of image and emotion into a unity of strangeness, beauty, and dread? It is part of the chapter in which Melville describes his ascent of the mainmast to loosen a skysail at midnight:

For a few moments I stood awe-stricken and mute. I could not see far out upon the ocean, owing to the darkness of the night; and from my lofty perch the sea looked like a great, black gulf, hemmed in, all round, by beetling black cliffs. I seemed all alone; treading the midnight clouds; and every second, expected to find myself falling—falling—falling, as I have felt when the nightmare has been on me.

I could but just perceive the ship below me, like a long narrow plank in the water; and it did not seem to belong at all to the yard, over which I was hanging. A gull, or some sort of sea-fowl, was flying round the truck over my head, within

a few yards of my face; and it almost frightened me to hear it;
it seemed so much like a spirit, at such a lofty and solitary
height.

It is not only the spectral sea-fowl here, flying round the masthead in the
darkness, which tells one that, in the progress from *Typee* to *Moby Dick*,
Melville has already passed the middle point.

If this holds for *Redburn* stylistically, it holds no less truly for its
substance and spirit. The outward subject of the book is a young boy's
first voyage as a sailor before the mast; its inward subject is the initiation
of innocence into evil—the opening of the guileless spirit to the
discovery of "the wrong," as James would say, "to the knowledge of it, to
the crude experience of it." The subject is a permanent one for literature,
of course, but it has also a peculiarly American dimension, and in just
this sense, not in any other, *Redburn* looks backward to a book like
Brockden Brown's *Ormond* as well as forward to *The Marble Faun* and to
so much of James himself. Wellingborough Redburn sets out from his
mother's house in a state of innocence like that before the Fall, a state
like that of Brown's Constantia Dudley or James's Maisie Farange, but
he has hardly gone a mile from home before the world's wickedness and
hardness begin to strip themselves before him. Man, Redburn quickly
finds, is a wolf to man. On the river boat his shabby indigence elicits no
compassion from the comfortable passengers, but only coldness and
disdain. He reaches the city and is very soon victimized by a rascally
pawnbroker, a pawnbroker who might have stepped out of *David
Copperfield* or *Cousin Pons*. He takes himself aboard the *Highlander* and
begins at once to be sworn at, pushed around, humiliated, and
persecuted by mates and sailors alike; and the dapper Captain Riga, who
had appeared so friendly in his cabin while the ship lay at anchor, now,
when poor unsophisticated Redburn attempts to address him as man to
man, flies into a rage and flings his cap at him.

Blows and hard words are mostly Redburn's lot on the *Highlander*,
yet he suffers not only from the inhumanity of men but from the
spectacle of their depravity generally. His feelings about the sailors
vacillate, it is true; as individuals he finds some of them generous and
friendly; but taking them in the lump, he is conscious chiefly of their
drunkenness, their profanity and obscenity, their indurated cynicism and
sneering misanthropy. All this accumulated evil, indeed, is focused so
concentratedly in the figure of one man, the sailor Jackson, as to raise

him to something like heroic stature, the stature at any rate of one of Schiller's Majestic Monsters. The first of Melville's full-length studies of "depravity according to nature," Jackson is stricken, symbolically, with a fatal disease—the penalty for his "infamous vices," as Redburn learns—but this does not keep him from being a pitiless bully and exercising an unchallenged and almost preternatural sway over the rest of the crew, who thus, in their pusillanimity, pay tribute to the principle of pure evil in him. He for his part feels nothing but malevolence toward them; nothing but malevolence toward Redburn, if only because he is young, handsome, and innocent; and indeed "he seemed to be full of hatred and gall against everything and everybody in the world." His enmity toward the boy sets the rest of the crew against him too, and Redburn begins to feel a compensatory hatred growing up in himself against them all; but meanwhile, day by day, his ears are assailed by the bitter talk of a man who is "spontaneously an atheist and an infidel," and who argues through the long night watches that there is "nothing to be believed; nothing to be loved, and nothing worth living for; but everything to be hated, in the wide world."

There is a touch of Svidrigailov or old Karamazov in this Jackson, and there is a touch of the Dostoyevskian also in Redburn's feeling that there was "even more woe than wickedness about the man." He is so impressive a figure, one sees, partly because so much of Melville's own bitterness and disbelief entered into his composition. Jackson is easily first among the personal embodiments of evil in this book, but in addition to him and to all the personages, and more overpowering than any of them, there is the infernal city of Liverpool, a near neighbor of the City of Destruction itself. That older allegory is bound to occur to one's mind in thinking of *Redburn* and Liverpool, but even so it was not until the nineteenth century that the great city, any great city, the great city *an sich*, could become just the kind of symbol it did become of human iniquity. In imagining Liverpool as he did, Melville was wholly at one with the deepest sensibility of his age, and in his wonderful series of Hogarthian evocations in the dark, begrimed, polluted streets, the great prisonlike warehouses, the squalid dwellings, the loathsome haunts of vice and crime, and the beggars, the quacks, the crimps, the peddlers who populate these infested purlieus like moral grotesques—in all this there is a power quite comparable to that with which Balzac's Parisian Inferno is rendered, or Baudelaire's *fourmillante cité*, the London of *Bleak House* and *Our Mutual Friend*, or the Dublin of *Ulysses*. Melville's Liverpool, too, like his Lima, is a City of the Plain.

In such a setting as this there is no mere enigma even in the one chapter of *Redburn* in which Melville seems to be indulging in deliberate mystification—the chapter in which he represents Redburn as being carried off to London on an unexplained errand by his new friend Harry Bolton and taken by him to "Aladdin's Palace." This is an Orientally luxurious pleasure-house of some ill-defined sort, where they spend a melodramatic night, and where Harry appears to lose most of his remaining funds at the tables. Aladdin's Palace is the opulent counterpart of the "reeking" and "Sodom-like" dens in Liverpool where Redburn's shipmates indulge their squalid vices; the walls of one room are hung with pornographic paintings to which Melville suggests various learned parallels, but most of these he himself invented as he composed the passage; and their real purpose, like that of the whole chapter, is to dramatize the horrified Redburn's feeling that "this must be some house whose foundations take hold on the pit," and that "though gilded and golden, the serpent of vice is a serpent still." He fails to see another stick or stone of London, and one more drop is thus added to his cup of disappointment; but his experience of evil has been extended in still another direction, and by the engaging Harry, too. The conflict between wishfulness and revulsion is evident enough. For the rest, though the chapter is not without a genuine vein of dreamlike intensity, it is vitiated as a whole by the kind of unnaturalness into which Melville so easily fell with such themes.

Meanwhile, *Redburn* abounds in the imagery not only of moral evil but of disease, disaster, and death. The voyage itself, here as elsewhere, is a metaphor of death and rebirth, of the passage from childhood and innocence to experience and adulthood; the crossing, to and fro, of a sea in the waters of which one dies to the old self and puts on a new. As if to enforce this intention irresistibly, the *Highlander's* voyage outward and the voyage home are both initiated by a scene of violent death. During the first long night watch that Redburn stands with his mates on the voyage out, he is terrified when all at once a sailor, suffering from delirium tremens, dashes up the scuttle of the forecastle and flings himself to his death over the bows of the vessel. The boy Redburn is then poetically identified with this sailor when he is made to occupy the dead man's bunk. Still more ghastly than this is the discovery, in the first dogwatch of the voyage homeward, that a Portuguese sailor who had been thrown, apparently dead drunk, into a bunk as they left port, is literally dead, and that his corpse is now flickering with a hideous phosphorescence. Neither incident, it appears, occurred on the actual voyage that the young Melville made; both are inventions, and all the more eloquent for being so.

Inventions, too, no doubt, are at least some of the other disastrous episodes of the voyage and of the stay in Liverpool: the collision between the *Highlander* and another vessel, in the darkness, which just fails to be fatal; the sighting of a dismantled, waterlogged schooner in the Irish Sea, with dead men lashed to the taffrail, the victims of storm and starvation (an echo, possibly, of *Arthur Gordon Pym,* but not an improvement on it); the murder of a prostitute at a bar in Liverpool by a drunken Spanish sailor; and the epidemic that, on the homeward voyage, destroys many of the inmates of the overcrowded, unwholesome steerage, and throws the refined cabin passengers into a cowardly panic of terror and selfishness. In these last scenes, as nowhere else in his work, Melville resorts to the symbolism of plague and pestilence that had proved, or was to prove, so expressive for a long series of modern writers, from Defoe and Poe to Thomas Mann; and though for him, as for most of them, the literal pestilence has a moral or spiritual reference, it is characteristic that for him, almost alone among such writers, it has a democratic and humanitarian reference also.

All these elements in *Redburn,* at any rate, are "symbolic" in the sense that, at their best, they are imagined and projected with an intensity that constantly pushes them beyond mere representation, and that makes them reverberate with a more than prosaic force in the reader's own imagination. Nothing like this had been true of *Typee* or *Omoo*: if there are symbols in those books, they are there only in the loose sense in which one would find them in any piece of writing that lifted itself even a little above the level of a mere record. The sense of symbol in *Redburn* is unmistakably more acute than in anything of Melville's that preceded *Mardi,* and moreover there are two or three points in the book at which one sees Melville moving toward an even franker and more direct form of symbolism, one which he himself would doubtless have called "allegorical," but which is far from being allegorical in the sense in which Yillah and Hautia had been. It is a question now, not of bodying forth emotional and intellectual experiences in deliberately poetic characters and fables, of elaborating dramatic symbols that have obvious analogies in the realm of thought and feeling. It is a question of endowing ordinary objects, ordinary incidents, with a penumbra of feeling and suggestion that imparts to them a symbolic character. One might describe these as antiromantic or shrunken symbols; they have something of the quality of what is called witty imagery, and they were to become more and more idiosyncratic for Melville.

One of them, here, is the old-fashioned glass ship which Redburn's father had brought home from France and which the boy's imagination had hovered over until the object converted his vague longings into a definite purpose of going to sea. On the very day on which he actually left home for his voyage, the little glass figurehead of a warrior had fallen from the bows of the ship into the waves below it, and there he still lies: "but I will not have him put on his legs again, till I get on my own." In very much the same vein of feeling is the old guidebook to Liverpool which, as we have seen already, had proved so helpful to Redburn's father in his perambulations about the city, but which now proves as misleading and even pervertive as every guidebook is that has had its day. Most striking of all, however, and happiest in its imaginative quality is the old gray shooting-jacket that Redburn's elder brother gives him as he sets out from home; the moleskin shooting-jacket with big horn buttons, long skirts, and many pockets, that brings down upon Redburn so much derision from fellow-passengers, shipmates, and Englishmen; which shrinks day by day, particularly after a rain, until he finds it more and more uncomfortable to wear; and which comes to be for him an obsessive emblem of his lost gentility and social humiliation. Redburn's shooting-jacket puts one in mind of that other shabby garment, the old clerk's overcoat in Gogol's famous tale, and indeed, in his characteristic preoccupation with clothing, especially shabby and uncomfortable clothing, Melville suggests the Russians more than any other English or American writer quite does. For the "insulted and injured" there is of course a natural metaphor in old, cheap, and ill-fitting clothes.

Bitter as the feeling in this is, however, and despite the underlying gravity of the symbolism generally, *Redburn* is anything but a lugubrious book as a whole, and it has probably never made any such impression on its readers: the current of animation and vivacity on which it is sustained is purely inspiriting; if this is "pessimism," it is pessimism of the most tonic sort. The book abounds in self-pity, certainly, but distinctions have to be made even here, and there is a kind of self-pity that is more bracing than what passes for restraint and austerity: on the whole, the self-pity in

Redburn is clearly of that order. Melville's feeling, moreover, for light and shade did not fail him in the writing of *Redburn* as it had done in the writing of *Mardi*. There is the familiar ballast of prosaic information, for one thing—the chapter, for example, on the furniture of the quarter-deck—and there is a good deal of Melville's characteristically smiling and low-toned humor. The account of Max the Dutchman, who has a sober and respectable wife in New York and an equally sober and respectable one in Liverpool, and whose wardrobe is kept in order by the launderings of both spouses—Max the Dutchman is in Melville's happiest vein. He had always had a taste for the burgherlike humor of the little Dutch masters—Teniers, Brouwer, Jan Steen—and in passages like this he approximates it, though in a softened form. In its richness of emotion and variety of tone, *Redburn* generally is the most likable of Melville's secondary books; and it is only because he was so rebelliously conscious how much higher he was capable of going that Melville could have spoken of it contemptuously as "beggarly *Redburn*."

Taken as a whole, *White-Jacket*, which he now went on to write, is something of a drop in quality after *Redburn*; it bears somewhat the same relation to that book as *Omoo* bears to *Typee*. Neither *Redburn* nor *White-Jacket*, and especially not the latter, was written with the concentrated conviction of Melville's whole nature: increasingly he was resentful of the necessities that forced him to write in what seemed to him an inferior strain. Both these books, he said in a letter, he had done simply as jobs, for the sake of making money, as other men are forced to saw wood, and at a time when what he earnestly desired was to write "those sort of books which are said to 'fail'." This, naturally, is a biographical fact, not a critical one, and we cannot be affected by Melville's own feeling in judging either *Redburn* or *White-Jacket*; but the biographical fact has an explanatory interest nevertheless. The earnest desire Melville expressed in his letter was soon to be fulfilled; meanwhile, he seems to have been writing at a murderous rate of speed, and *White-Jacket* itself appears to have been dashed off in the incredible space of two and a half months. It is little wonder that, in writing it, Melville should have lifted from other books not only information (as he had always done) but whole scenes and episodes, without always justifying the theft by improving on what he took. In at least one case he did so, but the symptoms of hurry and fatigue are all too evident elsewhere.

Hitherto he had intuitively succeeded in finding pretty much the true balance between narrative and factuality, between the imaginative and the informative, and in *White-Jacket* he continues to alternate the two—but now in what seems a relatively perfunctory and even wearied manner. The current of personal narrative is simply not full enough or strong enough to buoy up and float along the solid and sometimes rather lumpish blocks of straight exposition and description—straight information about the American navy generally and the individual battleship in particular. Not quite for the first time, but for the first time oppressively, one is conscious of the slight streak of pedantry that was always latent in Melville's passion for facts, and that when his imagination was not deeply engaged betrayed him into dullness and jejuneness. In proportion to the whole, one hears too much, in *White-Jacket*, about the gundeck and the berth-deck, the starboard watch and the larboard watch, the quarter-deck officers and the warrant-officers, and so on. In matters of organization and routine such as these Melville was not genuinely interested, or was interested only with the least creative facet of his imagination, and the result is that he largely fails to endow these things with imaginative life.

The book suffers too, more than the earlier books had done, from the humanitarian note that dominates it as it dominates no other work of Melville's. It is hardly worth saying that, on ethical grounds, one cannot fail to share Melville's indignation. Whatever the personal basis for it, he could not have taken firmer ground than he did when he cried out against "the social state in a man-of-war," the atrocious evil of flogging, and the like. All of it does the utmost credit to Melville's humanity. What was amiss was not this, certainly, but for the time being Melville's sense of form, his literary instinct. In speaking of *White-Jacket* one is tempted to paraphrase Flaubert's remark about *Uncle Tom's Cabin* and Negro slavery, and to ask: "Is it necessary to make comments on the iniquities of the Navy? Show them to me; that is enough." *White-Jacket* is not a novel, to be sure, but it is not a mere pamphlet either; it is an imaginative work of a very special and precarious sort, and it would have gained incalculably if Melville had made his protests far less insistent and less explicit, and if he had dramatized them much more. At least one of the flogging scenes, for example, seems terribly true, but none of them is comparable in repellent power to the one scene with which Dana, in *Two Years*, contents himself; and Melville dilutes the force of his protest partly by his repetitions of the shocking image and partly by his detailed comments on the evil. His moral passion, as so often happens, had asserted itself overaggressively at the expense of his inventive and dramatic gift.

It did not keep him, however, from continuing in *White-Jacket* the search for a right symbolic method that he had carried on in the two books that came before it. This search now led him, confusedly enough, in two directions, one of them a sterile, one a fruitful direction. It was an unhappy inspiration, as it was very probably an afterthought, that induced him to transform the man-of-war itself into the particular kind of symbol that the subtitle, "The World in a Man-of-War," indicates. From time to time as the book advances there are hints that the battleship *Neversink* is a kind of Microcosm of the universe; in one of the later chapters it is specifically remarked that "a man-of-war is but this old-fashioned world of ours afloat"; and finally Melville appends a short epilogue in which the analogy between a battleship and the Macrocosm is explicitly enforced. Just as the *Neversink* sails through the sea, so the earth sails through the air, "a fast-sailing, never-sinking world-frigate, of which God was the shipwright." But the port from which the Macrocosm sails is forever astern; unlike most battleships, that frigate sails under sealed orders, "yet our final haven was predestinated ere we slipped from the stocks at Creation." There are parallels, too, between the social arrangements on a man-of-war and the state of society itself, and though "we the people," like the common seamen in the Navy, suffer many abuses, the worst of our evils we blindly inflict on ourselves.

There are fine touches in this epilogue, like the strangely Kafkaesque suggestion that an abused sailor would appeal in vain, during this life, "to the indefinite Navy Commissioners, so far out of sight aloft." Yet on the whole the macrocosmic symbolism of the man-of-war world is as infelicitous in its way as the allegory of *Mardi* is in its. It is not only hackneyed in itself—the thought of Longfellow's Ship of State is dangerously near at hand—but treated just as Melville treats it, it is far too simply pictorial and its ethical bearing is made far too ponderously explicit. What is it indeed but a curiously belated, anachronistic example of what the sixteenth and seventeenth centuries would have called an Emblem—a highly pictorial allegory with a significance that is frankly and unequivocally enforced? Ships under full sail on calm or stormy seas appear from time to time in the sometimes charming cuts that illustrate the old emblem books, and there is an allegorical ship, allegorical of the soul and its destiny, in the third book of Quarles's *Emblems*. Melville felt a natural affinity, as some other writers of his time did, for the literature of the Baroque era, and sometimes it proved to have a genuinely quickening influence on him.

But the emblem in a nineteenth-century literary setting was as inappropriate as a sixteenth-century woodcut would have been as an illustration; it was not in those terms that Melville's problem would find its proper solution.

He was much closer to his own true vein in inventing the symbol that gives the book its title, the white jacket that, in lieu of a genuine pea jacket or grego, he represents his young hero, or rather "himself," as concocting out of an old duck shirt before the *Neversink* sets sail from Callao. He does so in order to protect himself from the boisterous weather they are sure to encounter as they round Cape Horn. "An outlandish garment of my own devising," the jacket is ample in the skirts, clumsily full about the wristbands, and of course white—"yea, white as a shroud." He darns and quilts the inside of it in the hope of making it truly waterproof; but, in spite of this, in rainy weather it proves to be as absorbent as a sponge, and thus "when it was fair weather with others, alas! it was foul weather with me." It is such an ungainly, eccentric garment that it brings down constant ridicule on the wearer's head, and worse than that, evokes a kind of superstitious hatred on the part of the other sailors. On one occasion they take White-Jacket himself to be the ghost of the cooper, lost overboard the day before, when they see him lying on the main-royalyard in the darkness; as time goes on, some of them are convinced that other deaths in the crew can be laid to the jacket, and White-Jacket himself begins to feel that the accursed garment has "much to answer for."

He has tried to persuade the first lieutenant to let him have some black paint to cover it with, but in vain. And this is a great part of his misery, for most monkey jackets are of a dark hue and keep their wearers from being too easily visible, especially at night. When, on the other hand, an officer wants a man for some particularly hard job, "how easy, in that mob of incognitoes, to individualize '*that white jacket*,' and dispatch him on the errand!" White-Jacket tries to free himself of the wretched thing by swapping it with a messmate and even by putting it up at auction, but no one will have it, and he begins to imagine that he will never be free of it until he rolls a forty-two-pound shot in it and commits it to the deep. This thought, however, is too much like the thought of his own death, and he refrains. But when the cruise is almost over, the jacket very nearly proves to be his death after all. White-Jacket is sent up the mainmast one night to reeve the halyards of a stun-sail, and while he is trying to do this he loses his balance and, entangled about the head by his jacket, falls rushingly from the yard-arm into the sea. Down he plunges, down into the deathlike waters of the deep. After some seconds, however, he shoots up again to the surface, and attempts to strike out toward the ship, but the fatal jacket, looped about him as it is, almost destroys him. He saves himself only by cutting himself out of it with a knife and ripping it up and down "as if I were ripping open myself." It sinks slowly before his eyes, and White-Jacket returns to life. He does so because he has in fact ripped open an aspect of himself, thrown it off, and allowed it to sink in the sea; the aspect of himself that is mere uniqueness and differentness, mere protective-unprotective self-assertion, easy to identify and individualize in any mob, and white, fatally white, as white as a shroud.

It is a magnificent symbol of the lesser Self, the empirical Self, the Ego; a far finer symbol for its purpose than that of the man-of-war for its, and it is so partly because it is homely and unhackneyed, partly because it is inexplicit, and partly because, though it has an interpretable meaning, that meaning remains elusive and slightly equivocal. The jacket was probably sheer invention on Melville's part, though he alleged in a letter to Dana that it was a real jacket. It does not matter in the least. In its setting the thing has the air of the only kind of reality that counts. Sheer invention, however, so far as Melville's external experience went, is certainly the great scene just alluded to, in which the jacket plays so nearly fatal a role. In literal fact no such mishap befell Melville on the *United States*. The ship's log is silent on the affair, and besides it has long been known that the whole scene is a rewriting of a passage in a little volume called *A Mariner's Sketches* by an old Yankee sailor named Nathaniel Ames, which had been published in Providence twenty years earlier.

It was a passage that was bound to catch Melville's attention as he read the book: the nightmarish image of falling to one's destruction from a high place had appeared before in his own writing, and what psychiatrists call hypsophobia was as characteristic for him as it was for Poe. He had reached the head of Taipi-Vai, according to his own story, by a series of horrifying falls from ledge to ledge of a dreamlike precipice; and in *Redburn*, in the passage already quoted, he represents his horror of "falling—falling—falling" when he is sent up to loosen the skysail. Harry Bolton on the voyage home suffers so terribly from this phobia that he refuses ever to climb the mast a second time, though he is permanently disgraced for it. And even earlier in *White-Jacket*, Melville or his fictional persona has nearly fallen to his death from the main-royalyard when the superstitious sailors below him suddenly lower the halyards. It takes no great penetration to detect in this recurring image the unconscious impulse to suicide, and the great scene in *White-Jacket* owes its inescapable power, as the scene of White-Jacket's near-flogging does, to the fact that, though it never occurred in the physical world, it did certainly occur in the inner one. The self-destructiveness in Melville expressed itself thus as well as in other ways.

Meanwhile, for all its limitations, *White-Jacket* has stretches of admirable writing in it, of which this scene of the fall from the yard-arm is one. It is already a famous case, but it remains an especially illuminating one, of Melville's genius for transmuting an uninspired model into something greatly expressive. Nathaniel Ames's own account of his fall from the futtock shrouds—oddly enough, it was on the same frigate, the *United States*—though it has several touches of strong realistic truth, is essentially as pedestrian as one would expect it to be if one heard it from the lips of the old seaman himself. Melville transformed it as Shakespeare sometimes transformed Holinshed or North's Plutarch: keeping the facts and the narrative order and even some of the details of feeling, but imparting rhythmicality, and a wonderfully connotative one, to what had had no rhythm at all; working small miracles of linguistic expressiveness ("the strong shunning of death shocked me through"); and intensifying the whole emotional value of the incident through an accompaniment of powerful images—"the speechless profound of the sea," "the maelstrom air," and "some inert, coiled fish of the sea." When he finds in Ames a matter-of-fact sentence like this:

> I kept going down, down, till it appeared to me that the seven fathoms and a half, (the depth of water at our anchorage,) had more than doubled since we let go our anchor;

Melville remakes it thus:

> The blow from the sea must have turned me, so that I sank almost feet foremost through a soft, seething, foamy lull. Some current seemed hurrying me away; in a trance I yielded, and sank deeper down with a glide. Purple and

pathless was the deep calm now around me, flecked by summer lightnings in an azure afar.

Much of the effect of this extraordinarily hypnotic passage is due to the delicate skill with which Melville avails himself of phonetic color—the color, here, of labials and sibilants especially and the closed sound of long *e*—but much also to the subtly responsive rhythms (conveying the delicious sense of movement downward through a liquid medium, in such gently protracted phrases as "through a soft, seething, foamy lull"), as well as to the synaesthetic use of a word like "lull" for an experience of the sense of touch, and the sudden shift from the sense of motion to the perception of color in the fine words, "purple" and "azure."

Admittedly this whole scene of the descent into the sea and the re-emergence from it is a rare peak in Melville's early prose; it is the finest writing in the ornate style that he did before *Moby Dick*, and one can account for it only by remembering that it sprang from a profound inward experience of life and death in conflict. But it is not the only passage of brilliant narrative writing in *White-Jacket*, despite the dead calm of many chapters. In an entirely different key, the key of relaxed and indulgent humor, the scene called "A Man-of-War College," in which the schoolmaster of the *Neversink* lectures to his flock of restless midshipmen on the refinements of naval strategy, is written with admirable ease and charm. In still another and a darker style, that of indignant, satirical caricature, Melville never went beyond the great scene of "The Operation"; the scene in which the pompous and unfeeling surgeon of the *Neversink*, Dr. Cadwallader Cuticle, performs an unnecessary amputation upon an injured foretopman, under which the wretched man dies. There is an inevitable suggestion of Smollett both in the name and in the character of the surgeon, as there is in the whole chapter; yet after all Melville did not write with the particular kind of harsh, brilliant, indefatigable speed and vigor one associates with the author of *Roderick Random*. Indeed, the passage has an essentially different quality from any of the scenes aboard the *Thunder* in that novel, a quality not so much of choleric energy as of mingled pity and detestation, revulsion and ruthlessness, humor and hatred. It would be easy, too, to say that Melville was writing in much the same style in which, for example, Rowlandson drew when he made his monstrous print of "The Amputation"; but the real feeling in Melville is in fact no more that of Rowlandson—broad, gross, and grotesque—than it is that of Smollett. It is a feeling in which anger at the spectacle of cruelty is underlain by a still stronger sorrow at the spectacle of evil generally.

On these more intangible grounds *White-Jacket* represents no retreat from or palliation of the insights expressed in *Redburn*. One must confess, in fact, that the later book is the more richly counterpointed, in a moral sense, of the two. The World in a Man-of-War is, at the one extreme, quite as black a world as that in a merchant vessel or a great seaport; it is a world, on the whole, "charged to the combings of her hatch-ways with the spirit of Belial and all unrighteousness." A world of which the ferocious Articles of War form the domineering code could hardly be other than a basically brutal and un-Christian one, and brutal and un-Christian, with its ultimate dedication to purposes of bloodshed and destruction, the microcosm of the *Neversink* is. What follows morally is what could be predicted: overbearing arrogance on the part of most of the officers, genteel rascality on the part of others, petty insolence even in the boyish midshipmen, and cringing subservience or sullen vindictiveness on the part of many of the sailors—for Melville, committed as he is to the rank and file as over against their superiors, cannot and will not represent the human reality as different from what he has found it in experience. He does not spare himself the task, painful though he obviously finds it, of hinting at "other evils, so direful that they will hardly bear even so much as an allusion"; evils that involve some of the common seamen in "the sins for which the cities of the plain were overthrown."

The portrait of Bland, the knavish master-at-arms, though it is less completely dramatized than that of Jackson, is at least as subtle analytically; and his well-bred, unvulgar, "organic" scoundrelism is both more inexplicable and more profound than Jackson's understandable blackguardliness. Yet morally speaking, despite all this, *White-Jacket* has a higher *relievo* and a more complex truth than *Redburn*. There is the moral relief of goodness in *Redburn* but it is too largely associated with passiveness and even effeminacy; Redburn himself remains too much the mere victim, embittered but not very resistant, and Harry Bolton is a more extreme case than he. The stage in *White-Jacket* is occupied by a much more richly representative cast of characters. Not all the officers are bullies or martinets. Mad Jack, a junior lieutenant, is a paragon of generous, manly seamanship, and Colbrook, the handsome and gentlemanly corporal of marines, has the extraordinary courage to intercede for White-Jacket when he comes so close to a flogging. Some of the midshipmen are "noble little fellows," and as for the common seamen, there is the self-respecting old Ushant, there is Nord the silent and meditative, and above and beyond all there is of course the "incomparable" and "ever-glorious" Jack Chase, the heroic captain of the maintop, a far more masculine image of virtue than the pathetic Harry. It is quite in keeping with his love for Jack Chase, moreover, that we should feel the vein of iron in White-Jacket as we never quite feel it in Redburn. Melville, as he wrote the book, had at least for the time recovered from the despairing mood of *Mardi* and from the largely resentful mood of *Redburn*. White-Jacket, it is true, would have gone to his death rather than submit to a flogging, but he would have done so in an act of protest; and in a later scene, when death by water would have come so easily, he has the still greater courage to cut himself out of his fatal garment and return to life.

DANIEL HOFFMAN

Moby-Dick: *Jonah's Whale or Job's?*

I

MYTH AS METAPHOR

"There are some enterprises in which a careful disorderliness is the true method," Melville writes in *Moby-Dick*. His curious phrase suggests the delicate balance he had to maintain between the multitudinous metaphors that poured forth from his imagination and the prefiguration which had to be applied to their arrangement. Melville, as Constance Rourke suggested, "used the familiar method of the legend-maker, drawing an accumulation of whaling lore from many sources, much of it from New England, some of it hearsay, some from books, including stories of the adventures of other ships encountered at sea, or further tales suggested by episodes within the main sequence of his story." Among those who have observed the fact, Matthiessen has said it best: "In his effort to endow the whaling industry with a mythology befitting a fundamental activity of man in his struggle to subdue nature, [Melville] came into possession of the primitive energies latent in words." Not only does Melville make his own metaphors and endow them with the universal qualities of myths, but he also draws deeply on the mythic formulations of experience already available to him. Although there are

From *Twentieth Century Interpretations of Moby-Dick*. Michael T. Gilmore, ed. Originally published in *Form and Fable in American Fiction*. (Charlottesville: University Press of Virginia, 1994) © 1961, 1989, 1994 by Daniel G. Hoffman. Reprinted by permission of the author.

dim prefigurations in his earlier romances of what he was to do in *Moby-Dick*, Melville found his mature purpose and the means of rites which Ahab as Anti-Christ performs on the quarter-deck. Then "Ahab's crazy quest seemed mine." But Ishmael discovers a deeper magic, a more potent source of supernatural energy, and dissolves this specious bond of Ahab's with a counter-ritual of his own. The brotherhood of violence to which Ahab bound him proves to be the self-destructive moral nihilism of selfhood uncontrolled. Freed by his discovery, in "A Squeeze of the Hand," of the organic unity of man with fellow-man, Ishmael wins his right to be the "sole survivor" of the final catastrophe. Cast up by the sea, he is saved by the coffin prepared for his boon companion Queequeg the cannibal, to whom the bonds of human love had bound him closest.

Opposed to the legend of the mighty hero are other mythical patterns in *Moby-Dick* which dramatize the contraries to Ahab's aggression against the inscrutable forces in the universe. The Hunter may be not only an aggressor but a Seeker, a seeker after truth. Opposed to Ahab's power and defiance is love. But love, to be an effective counter-principle, must find its proper object; should love turn inward, rather than embrace the "Not-Me," it becomes its own opposite, the wish for death. One of the manifestations of love in *Moby-Dick* occurs in versions of the myth of Narcissus, who, falling in love with his own image, destroyed himself. In the Narcissus myth, which Melville invokes in the very first chapter (and often again), the hunter becomes both a seeker and a solipsist. Yet it is the power of love alone, an outward-reaching love, that can overcome the wished-for death, as Ishmael but not Ahab learns.

When the hunt is for a whale who seems to embody divine power, when the Hunters and Seekers are also Rebels against divinity or candidates for repentance and redemption, it is inevitable that the Biblical legend of Jonah govern much of the metaphor and the action. In fact Melville introduces this myth into the narrative early too, taking from the Book of Jonah the text for Father Mapple's sermon. That Christian sermon states the ethical desiderata against which the fates of Ahab, Ishmael, and the rest are subsequently measured. Part of their fate is to relive aspects of Jonah's rebellion against God's Word, his incarceration in the whale, his being cast forth, and his redemption. Only Ishmael can reenact the entire myth; for the others, to each is given his own portion of Jonah's suffering, wisdom, and glory. These then are the executive metaphors from mythology and fulfilling it in the process of writing his greatest book. His mythical themes seem to leap fully-formed from his mind. We may observe that he draws together the mythical patterns of several cultures and of several levels within his own culture: the primitive ritual, the Greek myth, the Biblical legend, the folklore of supernatural dread and wonder (common to both the Old World and the New), and the specifically American folk traditions of comic glorification, of Yankee and frontier character. And in the "careful disorderliness" which is "the true method" of *Moby-Dick* these themes from myth, folklore, and ritual are ranged in a series of dialectical contrasts which dramatize and unify the several controlling tensions of the work.

Among these tensions the chief are those between the two examples of the hero. The contrary commitments of Ahab and Ishmael are dramatized in large part by their respective allegiances to certain heroes of Old World myth and of New World folklore. The narrative of the hunt embodies the seminal myth of a divinely-endowed hero who in hand-to-hand combat rids his people of the evil monster that was their scourge. Ahab appears to belong in the company in which Ishmael jocularly enrolls himself: among Perseus, Theseus, and Saint George. (Ishmael maintains that Cetus, the Medusa and the dragon, being sea-creatures, were necessarily whales.) But Ahab in fact differs from these prototypical figures in being a false culture-hero, pursuing a private grievance (rather than a divine behest) at the expense of the mankind in his crew. He is more properly a Faust who has sold his soul to the devil (who is aboard as Fedallah the fire-worshipper). A Faust who commands and enchants his followers becomes, as Ahab does, a Satan, a sorcerer, an Anti-Christ.

The lowly sailor, contrarily, is humanely adaptable and receptive to experience. Ishmael's style, the doubly comic and fearful cast of his imagination, and his metamorphic career all relate him to the qualities of the American folk character. His own involvement in the adventure he records takes the unsought but intrinsic form of initiation and rebirth. Indeed, for all aboard the *Pequod* the voyage is one of search and discovery, the search for the ultimate truth of experience. But each seeker can make only those discoveries his own character has preordained as possible for him. Ishmael's initiation is revealed through the pattern of the hunt whose object becomes known only when the crew is welded to their mad commander's purpose by the magical folklore which give this prodigious book much of its inner coherence.

The oppositions within the romance of the claims of aggression and passivity, of hostility and acceptance, of defiance and of submission to the "Divine Inert," are consistently proposed and elaborated by these masterful myth-symbols. The interstices of the action are braced by the enactment of rituals—among the most important are the "marriage" of Ishmael and Queequeg, the cannibal's worship of his idol, Father Mapple's sermon and the cook's, Ahab's black mass on the quarter-deck, Ishmael's cleansing of his soul in the spermaceti, and the final annihilating catastrophe. The work is yet almost everywhere saved from becoming what Melville shunned as "a hideous and intolerable allegory" by his insistence upon tangible fact: the reality of an actual ship and live whales, of a particular captain and his crew, and the documentation which makes *Moby-Dick* a guide to all of the operations of the whaling industry.

II

A Voyage to Nineveh

In the world of *Moby-Dick* nothing exists without its opposite and no vision which fails to encompass both poles of every contrast can embrace the truth. The qualities Melville dramatized through the Narcissus myth are necessarily in tension with their opposites, and those qualities inhere in another legendary nexus of images: the Jonah story. This theme is early introduced by Father Mapple's sermon in chapter 9. When Narcissus as Seeker leaned toward "the mild image in the fountain," Jonah as Rebel tries to flee by water from the command of God. Where Narcissus proves a solipsist, the rebel Jonah at last acknowledges the God beyond himself. In consequence Jonah is not, like Narcissus, a suicide, but is reborn, literally resurrected from his death inside the whale. These experiences of Jonah's prove to be prototypes of several adventures suffered not only by Ishmael and Ahab but also by the harpooners Tashtego and Queequeg and by the demented cabin-boy Pip.

It is essential that we recognize these not only as Biblical parallels but also as the enactments of the ritual significance of the Jonah story itself. That story, as William Simpson demonstrated in *The Jonah Legend* (London, 1899), is in fact the account of an initiation ceremony in which the candidate for admission to divine knowledge at first ceremonially rebels against submission to the divine behest, the "Not-Me"; then undergoes a symbolic mock-death in the whale's belly (actually, a vault below the floor of the temple);[1] and emerges reborn into the cult or priesthood.

Melville, writing half a century before Simpson, yet had access to the very evidence the later theologian would, with the help of Frazer's anthropology, systematize into his ritual interpretation. Drawing on both Pierre Bayle's *Historical and Critical Dictionary* and John Kitto's recently issued *Cyclopedia of Biblical Literature*, Melville found the very rationalistic hypotheses which the later theologian would use to support his contention that the Biblical Jonah legend was in fact a late variant of an ancient initiation ritual. These two sources of Melville's take opposite views of the same evidence (it is probable that Kitto drew on Bayle, disputing the Frenchman's skepticism, for his articles on "Jonah" and "Whale"). Melville mined whole paragraphs from both, sportively adopting the very rationalizations of the legend which the Frenchman proposed and which the pious encyclopedist had been at pains to discredit.

Melville, however, can make the descent into the whale just as literal as it seems in the Book of Jonah, as he does when Tashtego falls into the severed head of a dead sperm. Or he can describe the *Pequod* in similes suggesting the ship itself as a whale: "A cannibal of a craft"—as though she would swallow her crew—"tricking herself forth in the chased bones of her enemies," her bulwarks "garnished like one continuous jaw, with the long sharp teeth of the sperm whale," and her tiller "carved from the long narrow jaw of her hereditary foe." The similitude is already established in Father Mapple's text: "Beneath the ship's waterline, Jonah feels the heralding presentiment of that stifling hour, when the whale shall hold him in the smallest of his bowels' wards."

The conventional Christian interpretation of Jonah proposes his "death" and resurrection after three days in the whale as a prefiguration of Christ's rising. Melville consistently presents Ahab, his Anti-Christ, in the guise of an unrepentant Jonah. Ahab's disobedience of God's commands foredooms the voyage;[2] his aggressive will, we recognize, is in flight from truth rather than possessing it. His godless purpose provokes the elements themselves at the *Pequod*'s first pursuit of a whale. As they strike the whale, the storm strikes them; the ship looms through the mist and the frightened boat's crew cast themselves into the sea. But where Jonah confessed his apostasy and the crew threw him overboard, Ahab's "confession" on the quarter-deck puts his entire crew in league with him. The Anti-Christ is at this stage an Anti-Jonah, welcoming the catastrophe his own mad pride had created. Father Mapple had warned, "Delight—top-gallant delight is to him, who acknowledges no law or lord, but the Lord his God, and is only a patriot to heaven." This delight Ahab can never know, who blindly refuses to disobey himself. But Ahab meets his end as though it were a triumph; although he dies, Moby Dick has proved to be the "outrageous strength, with an inscrutable malice sinewing it; whether agent or principal," which Ahab hates, and in death Ahab merges at last with the uncontrollable power he pressed his pulse against when the corpusants blazed above him. Even some part of Jonah's delight is his after all: "And eternal delight and deliciousness will be his, who coming to lay him down, can say with his final breath—O Father!—Known to me chiefly by Thy rod—mortal or immortal, here I die." For the Hebraic-Calvinistic God of the Nantucket sailors' Bethel *is*, in the end, patristic, unknowable power. Compounded of heretical apostasies though Ahab's woe-reaping monism may be, he is yet on his own terms triumphant in defeat, acknowledging the justice of his dreadful punishment. But Ahab's terms are those of the sterile, regressive, annihilation-seeking solipsist. Having made himself into a destructive machine, he must perish without hope of resurrection.

Ishmael's original disobedience would consist in the "damp, drizzly November in his soul," the denial of life that brought him, too, to the *Pequod*'s wharf. (The sketch of the blacksmith, chapter 112, suggests that this death-wish is a universal motive.) Ishmael had said "The world's a ship on its passage out." He was in the boat that chased the first whale in the storm, and when the *Pequod* loomed out of the mist he too leapt into the sea. "Saved" by the ship, the *Pequod* for him becomes the whale it so curiously resembles. When it sinks, he is cast forth as Jonah was spewed from the mouth of the fish.

Although Ishmael more completely than the rest enacts Jonah's initiatory ritual, he does so in the presence not of Jonah's God but of Job's. Jonah's God, as Matthew 12:40 tells us, becomes God the Merciful Father of Jesus: "For as Jonas was three days and three nights in the heart of the earth." And the next verse prophesies that "The men of Nineveh shall rise in judgment with this generation, and shall condemn it: because they repented at the preaching of Jonas." When we compare Father Mapple's sermon to the Book of Jonah we are struck by Melville's suppression of the sequel to Jonah's deliverance from the whale; his Jonah does not propose to God vengeance against the sinners of Nineveh, nor is he chastened by the parable of the gourd, illustrating God's infinite mercy.

The fifth "Extract" is especially significant: "In that day, the Lord with his sore, and great, and strong sword, shall punish Leviathan the piercing serpent, even Leviathan that crooked serpent, and he shall slay the dragon that is in the sea" (Isa. 21:1). Here is biblical support for both Ishmael's contention that whalemen are the culture-heroes of antiquity and for Ahab's contention of his self-appointed destiny. It is of course the fatality of Ahab's hubris that he sees himself as the lordly avenger slaying the tangible shape of evil. But Ishmael, just after the quarter-deck, declares Ahab (in chapter 41) to be an "ungodly old man, chasing with curses a Job's whale round the world." After Ishmael has endured the annihilation Ahab willed, he begins his epilogue with the words of Job's messengers of destruction: "And I only am escaped alone to tell thee."

But who is "thee," and what message is Ishmael alone escaped to tell? He survives to preach to *us*, his Nineveh, as Father Mapple had said of Jonah who "did the Almighty's bidding. And what was that, shipmates? To preach the Truth to the face of Falsehood! That was it!"

Yet Ishmael's "Truth" is neither the submission of Jonah to God's will nor the still more Christian humility Father Mapple proposed as "top-gallant delight." How far Ishmael-Melville was from accepting the "Divine Inert" as his guide to this world is apparent from the contrast between Ishmael and Pip. For Pip's actions parallel Jonah's being cast away and Christ's resurrection, but at the cost of his accommodation to any life in this world. In a chapter titled "The Castaway" we learn how little Pip on his first whale chase had leapt in terror into the sea and was abandoned as Stubb pursued the whale. "The intense concentration of self in the middle of such a heartless immensity, my God! who can tell it?" When saved by the ship,

> the little negro went about the deck an idiot.... The sea had jeeringly kept his finite body up, but drowned the infinite of his soul. Not drowned entirely, though. Rather carried down alive to wondrous depths where strange shapes of the unwarped primal world glided to and fro before his passive eyes.... He saw God's foot upon the treadle of the loom, and

spoke it; and therefore his shipmates called him mad. So man's insanity is heaven's sense.

Pip's resurrection is entirely spiritual—his very name, Pip, for Pippin, suggests Matthew 13:38, "the good seed are the children of the kingdom." Losing his earthly senses, he participates in glory. In his gibberish he plays Fool to Ahab's Lear; in his sanctity, Good Angel to Ahab's Faust. Unheeded, Pip yet brings the New Testament God of Mercy and Transfiguration before the mind that conceives only of the Old Testament God of Wrath, vengeance and destruction. "Hands off that holiness!" Ahab cries, acknowledging the godliness in Pip that he has inverted and denied in himself. Ishmael may have Pip's transcendent glory in mind when he says, at the end of "The Castaway," "In the sequel of the narrative it will then be seen what like abandonment befell myself." Pip is in glory already; Ishmael, saved like Jonah from the whale, has yet to endure his span of life with the knowledge of God won at last by all his senses from experience of that whale. And the whale, as he had said, was "a Job's whale."

Tashtego's deliverance was more literally Jonah-like, since his peril was to have fallen into the head of a whale. Where Pip is spiritually "saved," the redemption of Tashtego is emphatically physical. Queequeg leaps overboard, knife in hand, cuts his way into the now sinking head, and by dint of "agile obstetrics," rescues Tashtego "in the good old way, head-first," in "a running delivery." This is but one of Queequeg's several acknowledgements of the divine law of love which makes him, at life's risk, assume responsibility for his fellow-man—first a bumpkin on a New Bedford schooner, later Ishmael himself; and, in the end, Queequeg proffers the coffin prepared for his sickness as a life-preserver with 30 life-lines, for the entire crew. Tashtego's rebirth from the whale keeps the Jonah imagery afloat in mid-passage, but it is focused throughout on Ahab's rebellion and Ishmael's survival. Queequeg is the agent both of Tashtego's delivery and of Ishmael's. But the cannibal's part in Ishmael's "delivery" is not merely to provide the coffin-lifebuoy, important as that is. Queequeg's love redeems Ishmael from the fatal isolation which had led him to choose Ahab's ship for his journey away from his self. He must lose himself to find himself. His love for Queequeg makes this possible, and qualifies Ishmael, alone of Ahab's oathbound crew, to dissever the bonds of hatred and vengeance and so qualify for survival from the annihilation that Ahab willed for all the rest.

III

GOD'S WHALE

Father Mapple's sermon early proposed the Christian ethic by which all subsequent actions are measured. How cruelly inapplicable this transcendent ethic is to the microcosm of the *Pequod* is dramatized in its seeming parody, the cook's sermon to the sharks. Stubb, the second mate, has killed a whale and must have the cook prepare him a steak for supper. Venting his vein of Mike Fink's frontier humor, the mate bullies the old Negro into preaching a sermon to the sharks swarming about the whale's carcass, "mingling their mumblings with his own mastications." The sermon is comic in the fashion of frontier dialect humor. "Your woraciousness, fellow-critters, I don't blame ye so much for: dat is natur, and can't be helped; but to gobern dat wicked nature, dat is de pint. You is sharks, sartin, but if you gobern de shark in you, why den you be angel...." "Well done, old Fleece, that's Christianity," cried Stubb.

Father Mapple's Christianity is meaningless in such a sharkish world. Only Pip, whose soul did not know the savagery necessary to the true whaler, the mortal man, can attain the selflessness of the Sermon on the Mount. The only other practicing Christian on the *Pequod* is the first mate, Starbuck. And he is described as suffering "the incompetence of mere unaided virtue or right-mindedness." Although physically no coward, the mate "cannot withstand those more terrific, because more spiritual terrors, which sometimes menace you from the concentrating brow of an enraged and mighty man." Living by his own code of Christian charity, he yet fails in what Ishmael presents to us as a higher law: active rebellion against active evil. Starbuck alone has the temporal authority, intelligence, and moral perception to overthrow Ahab's wicked tyranny and thus save all the crew. But he lacks the power to meet power with power; twice he might kill Ahab yet cannot pull the trigger, cannot let fall the rope; twice he might raise a mutiny, yet fails at the quarter deck and fails at the last chase, just as he always fails to dissuade Ahab from madness. Starbuck's unfulfilled duties are made plain by the interpolated fable of "The Town-Ho's Story" in which a subordinate's rebellion against a tyrannous mate is given divine sanction—by Moby Dick.

Nature does not accommodate or condone the failure to meet amoral force with force, what though power itself corrupt. Nature,

God's own creation, is not pure, but sharkish, vulturish, cannibalistic, horrible. And Ishmael, we have been told, knows himself a cannibal, ever ready to rebel against even his savage king. Christianity as Melville knew it was unequal to the needs his faith must fulfill. On one side it led to the repression of Eros, the worship of force, to Ahab's emasculation of humanity; on the other, to Starbuck's ineffectual passivity or to the super-human acceptance of the Divine Inert—Pip's mindless purity, which proves effeminate, passive, deathlike.

What faith Melville proposes through Ishmael's initiation is of course determined by the nature of his God. In the rituals of non-Christian worship and in the entire constellation of legends, superstitions, and beliefs about the whale we may find at last the lineaments of Deity in *Moby-Dick*.

To find his God, his father, had been Ahab's quest; his method he foretold in saying "All visible objects, man, are but as pasteboard masks.... If man will strike, strike through the mask!" Ahab's violence, projecting itself through the mask of appearances, never doubts that anything but itself lurks there: Narcissus as avenger.

But once in this book, though, Ishmael does see what lies behind the pasteboard mask. In his bedchamber at the Spouter Inn was "a papered fireboard representing a man striking a whale." Queequeg's first act on entering—before he even knows that Ishmael is in the room—is to remove this paper screen, and, there between the sooty firedogs, *he himself put the image of his own god*. The pasteboard mask conceals nothing that man has not put there.

Queequeg's idol is a black figurine named Yojo, who later counsels the cannibal to let Ishmael choose the ship of their adventure. After they have heard Father Mapple preach together, Ishmael, by now "married" to his friend, "must turn idolator," kindle Yojo's fire, and salaam to the pagan deity. What I take all this to mean is that the source of redemptive love is, for Melville, a divinity pre-Christian[3] and pre-rational. (This is why Queequeg invokes Yojo before being aware of Ishmael's presence.) But Yojo, the pagan love-god, is not the creator of the universe. The white whale seems as close as we can come to touching that power and awful beauty.

Yet neither is Moby Dick God; he is God's whale—and Job's whale. Ahab mistook God's power for God's essence, and heaped on that white hump "the intangible malignity which has been from the beginning ... all the subtle demonisms of life and thought." To Ishmael, however, the most terrifying aspect of the whale's whiteness is "a colorless all-color of atheism," the ever-present possibility of cosmic nothingness, in which "the palsied universe lies before us a leper." All of Ishmael's explorations of the attempts made in art, science, folklore and myth, to define the whale are a contradictory labyrinth of suppositions which only his own experience can verify. And that experience proves the white whale unknowable to the last. If, then, we cannot know God's greatest handiwork, how can we know the God that made him?

On this reef many an interpreter of *Moby-Dick* has foundered. It seems hard to resist Ahab's incantatory power and not agree with him, that the white whale is indeed the immanent God of this work, even though one reject Ahab's definition of His nature. But Moby Dick is no more the God of *Moby-Dick* than Leviathan is the God of the Book of Job. The inscrutable whale, titanic in power, lovely in motion, ubiquitous in space, immortal in time, is the ultimate demonstration and absolute convincement of all anarchic, individualistic, egotistical, human doubt that there is a God beyond the powers of man to plumb. Melville's God lies beyond even the Gospel truths. He is Job's God, not Jonah's prefiguration of Christ's rising. That is why Ishmael ends his tale with the words of the messengers of calamity.

It is hard to unmingle the knowledge of God's essence from the knowledge of His power. Ahab must grasp the chain-link to feel the living lightning against his own pulse, power participating in power. Ishmael, too, touches the will of deity by an act which the linked analogies of his metaphoric mind makes analogous to the will of godhead. This act is the weaving of the sword-mat (ch. 47). Just before the first whale was sighted, Ishmael and Queequeg together wove a mat to protect their boat. Ishmael's own hand was the shuttle; Queequeg drove a wooden "sword" between the threads to straighten the woof. Ishmael elaborates this scene in the manner of a Puritan preacher, making an extended conceit from homely images of common labor; as he speaks here of the most urgent philosophic problem of the book, a rather long quotation must be introduced:

> ... it seemed as if this were the Loom of Time, and I myself were a shuttle mechanically weaving and weaving away at the Fates. There lay the fixed threads of the warp subject to but one single, ever returning, unchanging vibration, and that vibration merely enough to admit of the crosswise

interblending of other threads with its own. This warp
seemed necessity; and here, thought I, with my own hand I
ply my own shuttle and weave my own destiny into these
unalterable threads. Meanwhile, Queequeg's impulsive,
indifferent sword, sometimes hitting the wood slantingly, or
crookedly, or strongly, or weakly, as the case might be; and by
this difference in the concluding blow producing a
corresponding contrast in the final aspect of the completed
fabric; this savage's sword, thought I, which thus finally
shapes and fashions both warp and woof; this easy, indifferent
sword must be chance—aye, chance, free will, and
necessity—no wise incompatible—all inter-weavingly
working together. The straight warp of necessity, not to be
swerved from its ultimate course—its very alternating
vibration, indeed, only tending to that; free will still free to
ply her shuttle between given threads; and chance, though
restrained in its play within the right lines of necessity, and
sidewise in its motions directed by free will, though thus
prescribed to by both, chance by turns rules either, and has
the last featuring blow at events.

At the savage lookout's first cry "There she blows!" "the ball of free will
dropped from my hand."
   Ishmael's quest from the beginning is to seek out and read the
pattern of the loom. The opening chapter is called "Loomings"; the pun
on "weavings" and the nautical term for something hidden below the
horizon coming into view is but the first hint of Ishmael's comedic
acceptance of what Father Mapple's hymn calls the "terrible" and the
"joyful" in his earthly life. The weaving image (though somewhat
contrived in the sword-mat passage) itself represents both the creative
and dynamic elements in Ishmael's view of the cosmos. The loom is still
a-weaving, the pattern ever emergent, never complete. Such a view is
directly antithetical to Ahab's rigid and mechanical conception of his
destiny: "This whole act's immutably decreed.... I am the Fates'
lieutenant." Ishmael's loom metaphor knits together the clusters of
images involving lines, ropes, and shrouds, realistically present on a
sailing-ship but imaginatively made to ply the loom of Fate on which
each thread adds its color and direction to the grand design. "What
depths of the soul Jonah's deep sealine sound!" preached Father Mapple;

"Shipmates, it is a two-stranded lesson." The strands of life and of death appear in later lines, especially "the magical, sometimes horrible whaleline." "All men live enveloped in whale-lines. All men are born with halters round their necks." This is the line that tossed Pip overboard, entangled Fedallah, slew Ahab. Complementary to this death-line is the lifeline, the "monkey-rope" that ties seamen together. "So that for better or for worse, we two, for the time, were wedded; and should poor Queequeg sink to rise no more, then both usage and honor demanded that instead of cutting the cord, it should drag me down in its wake. So, then, an elongated Siamese ligature united us." The life-line is at once a love-link, a death-line, and an umbilicus. These cords are intermingled again as the harpooner's line tangles with the trailing umbilicus of new-born whale cubs. Love and death are imaged together when Ishmael regards the whale-line in its tub as "a prodigious wedding-cake to present to the whales." Even the weather contributes to the loomed design as "mingling threads of life are woven by warp and woof; calm crossed by storm, a storm for every calm.... Where lies the final harbor, whence we unmoor no more?"

That final harbor is as hidden from mortal navigators as the "insular Tahiti" of unfallen delight, once pushed off from never to be found again. Yet Pip has moored there. For when afloat on the terrifying sea "He saw God's foot upon the treadle of the loom, and spoke it.... So man's insanity is heaven's sense; and wandering from all mortal reason, man comes at last to that celestial thought, which, to reason, is absurd and frantic; and weal or woe, feels then uncompromised, indifferent as his God."[4]

Indifferent, that is, to mortal weal or woe; these are no concern of the God who set down "WHALING VOYAGE BY ONE ISHMAEL" in "the grand programme of Providence that was drawn up a long time ago." For that God—Ishmael's God—is himself creative power, subsuming all the fragmentary deities men erect in his partial image: Ahab's and Fedallah's destructive Force, Queequeg's all-fructifying love, Pip's and Bulkington's Christian Absolute, the Divine Inert. Transcending the sum of these is the ever-emergent God of Life and Death, revealing Himself through Nature, the Work that he creates. Moby Dick, the greatest of his handiwork, is the principle of Godhead *in* Nature. This God does not allow (as Richard Chase among others reminds us) either a tragic or a Christian resolution of man's fate; Melville's view does indeed resemble at some points Spinoza's (as Newton Arvin has suggested), that man's happiness consists in knowing his true place in nature. Far more deeply than the literary naturalists of the end of his century, he comprehends in the cosmos a God of energy whose moral laws, if they exist, transcend all human divination. Yet Melville's God of Force is not like Zola's or Dreiser's or Crane's, Himself a mere machine; in *Moby-Dick* that view is Ahab's blindness. Melville posits not immutable mechanical law but the universal vitality of Nature, embracing death as preludial to rebirth. In this he comes close to Whitman, though Melville cannot rest as easily as Whitman did with the facile and unstable resolution of all dilemmas proposed in "Song of Myself."

As close as Melville comes to a resolution in *Moby-Dick* is in a chapter few critics have noticed, "A Bower in the Arsacides." Here the images of the white whale and the weaver-god come together in Ishmael's mind, and here too is the image of the machine—indeed, a modern industrial factory. Such images define the limits of Ahab's will, for his "path ... is laid with iron rails, whereon [his] soul is grooved to run"; but here Ishmael sees the mechanical in its right relation to cosmic truth. These images of whale, weaver, and machine occur in Ishmael's mind as he recalls a previous voyage when he visited the island where a whale's white skeleton forms a chapel decked with vines. This is a context independent of both Ahab, his own crippling death-wish, and Queequeg, his own regressive infantilism. One last extended excerpt will repay our consideration:

> The industrious earth beneath was as a weaver's loom, with a gorgeous carpet on it, whereof the ground-fine tendrils formed the warp and woof, and the living flowers the figures.... Through the lacings of the leaves, the great sun seemed a flying shuttle weaving the unwearied verdure. Oh, busy weaver!—pause!—one word!—whither flows the fabric? what palace may it deck? wherefore all these ceaseless toilings? Speak, weaver!—stay thy hand!—but one single word with thee! Nay—the shuttle flies—the figures float from forth the loom; the freshet-rushing carpet for ever slides away. The weaver-god, he weaves; and by that weaving is he deafened, that he hears no mortal voice; and by that humming we, too, who look on the loom are deafened; and only when we escape it shall we hear the thousand voices that

speak through it. For even so it is in all material factories. The spoken words that are inaudible among the flying spindles; those same words are plainly heard without the walls, bursting from the opened casements. Ah, mortal! then, be heedful; for so, in all this din of the great world's loom, thy subtlest thinkings may be overheard afar.

Now, amid the green, life-restless loom of that Arsacidean wood, the great, white, worshipped skeleton lay lounging— a gigantic idler. Yet ... the mighty idler seemed the cunning weaver; himself all woven over with vines ... but himself a skeleton. Life folded Death; Death trellised Life; the grim god wived with youthful Life, and begat him curly-headed glories.

Here process is mechanical; in the mortal activity of becoming, the Word is drowned. That activity is only the effect, not the Source, of divine energy. The skeleton whale—white—"seemed the cunning weaver"—for on this island as well as on the *Pequod*'s ocean (and in Job) we can come no nearer to the Source than to behold the greatest of His works. It is the loom of this whale's dead bones, interwoven with life, that Ishmael measured with a ball of twine and tattooed upon his own right arm.

How then can we stand beyond the walls of the factory to hear the Word that its mechanical humming drowns? How fathom the pattern in the endless fabric of Life and Death? One way is amply plain—by stepping outside of the world of process, we, with the death of our human senses, may behold the grand design. But Ishmael at last will be redeemed from such a Redemption. He wills himself to *live*. And what truth he has survived to tell us we may find written on the whale's brow, "pleated with riddles." These are unriddled on the whale's talisman, the doubloon.

On that coin "the keystone sun" came through the zodiac at "the equinoctal point of Libra," the scales. And the coin was made in Ecuador, "a country planted in the middle of the world," named for the equator, and was minted "in the unwaning clime that knows no autumn." None of these visible facts had been *felt* by any of the doubloon's beholders; each save Pip sought the phantom of life and grasped only "his own mysterious self." Pip, already at the Resurrection, is beyond the doubloon's gift of wisdom, which Ishmael alone receives.

The scales of Libra are no. doubt those "scales of the New Testament" by which Ishmael weighed his mortal lot at the beginning and found it tolerable. What is important here is that at *their* point in the heavens the "keystone sun" enters the universe. But the conception of balance is not only transcendent; represented by the pagan zodiac, the geographic equator, and the physical reality of that "unwaning clime" halfway up the Andes, the idea necessarily extends to *that wholeness which is comprised of both the halves*: both hemispheres, both peaks and valleys, both winter and summer, both hot and cold—both love and death, highest good and deepest evil, mortality and immortality. Unlike Starbuck's *mediocritas*, this balanced, doubled vision encompasses all extremes and thereby asserts its absolute stability. It is godlike. To attain it and survive, Ishmael must drown his Ahab and his Queequeg. But first he must have acknowledged them.

Like the builders of the Cathedral of Cologne, Melville leaves the true copestone of *Moby-Dick* to posterity. Had he imposed perfect form upon his partial vision of the truth he sought, he would have falsified his own achievement. This is an intrinsic principle of Melville's aesthetic. Yet in *Moby-Dick* the incandescence of the metaphoric linkage we have observed does project successfully the unification of experience. It does this by creating autonomously the world within which its own meanings are true. This world is braced and pinioned by the primitive sanctions and mythic values, the supernatural forces and ritualistic acts that we have traced. And yet, as distant as such materials would seem to be from the workaday life of Melville's time, in *Moby-Dick* he elaborates almost all of the levels of experience, as well as of mythic feeling and metaphoric thought, which might typify his culture and his time. From savagery to spindle-factories, from Old Testament Calvinism to the gamecocks of the frontier, from demonology to capitalism, the imagery of American life on every level sinews the entire book. Melville's view of life is doubtless a less catholic view than we find in Dante, or in his favorite author Shakespeare, or in Cervantes. Yet his is the greatest work by an American imagination for the same reasons that theirs are the greatest works of European Christendom. *Moby-Dick* most profoundly expresses the aspirations and the limitations of the culture as well as the individual genius that produced it. And that culture has, thus far, given us fewer tragic heroes and transcendent Christians than individualists alienated from their pasts, striving to discover those "humanities" which yet may bind them to "the magnetic circle of mankind."

NOTES

1. In the prefatory "Etymology" Melville cites as one origin of the word *whale* the Danish *hvalt*, "arched or vaulted."

2. In his earlier assault against God's command (on the previous voyage) the whale had given him warning of God's will by *swallowing only his leg*. Ahab is maddened rather than forewarned.

3. Yojo is the same color as the whale's phallus and as that priapic idol which Queen Maachah worshipped and Asa, her son, destroyed and "burnt for an abomination at the brook of Kedron, as darkly set forth in the fifteenth chapter of the first book of Kings" (ch. 95; cf. I Ki. 15:13). Melville surely invented this obscure comparison (the Bible does not even darkly hint at the color of the Queen's idol) because at the very place where Asa burnt the phallic image, Judas betrayed Jesus (John: 18:1–5). Christianity and the sensual Eros are mutually exclusive in *Moby-Dick*.

4. Ahab saw his pattern too, "when God's burning finger [was] laid upon the ship; when His 'Mene, Tekel, Upharsin' [was] woven into the shrouds and cordage." Then Ahab embraced the corpusants, as though to knot the design against the unraveling of chance.

Chronology

1819	Born in New York City to Allan Melvill and Maria Gansevoort Melvill, August 1.
1830	Father, Allan Melvill, bankrupt; family moves to Albany.
1832	Allan Melvill dies; an "e" is added to the name Melville in order to make a connection to the Scottish Melville clan.
1838	Melville enrolls at Lansingburgh Academy to study engineering and surveying.
1839	Melville sails for Liverpool aboard the *St. Lawrence* and returns four months later.
1840	Melville travels to Illinois seeking employment, visits Uncle Thomas's farm, returns home, unsuccessful.
1841	Melville sails from New Bedford, Massachusetts, aboard the whaler *Acushnet* on January 3.
1842	Melville and Richard Tobias Greene jump ship in the Marquesas Islands. In July, Melville sails aboard the whaler *Lucy Ann* for Tahiti, is jailed briefly in Tahiti for participation in a crew rebellion, sails on *Charles and Henry* to Hawaii.
1843	Melville works in bowling alley and calico shop in Honolulu before enlisting in the U.S. Navy and sails back to Boston on the *United States*.

1844	Melville is discharged from the Navy in Boston in October.
1846	Melville publishes *Typee*. Gansevoort dies.
1847	Melville publishes *Omoo*. He marries Elizabeth Shaw (Lizzie) and settles in New York City.
1848	Melville publishes *Redburn*. He journeys to Europe.
1849	Melville publishes *Mardi*. His son Malcolm is born.
1850	Melville publishes *White-Jacket*. He purchases "Arrowhead," a farm outside Pittsfield, Massachusetts, meets and becomes friendly with Nathaniel Hawthorne.
1851	Melville publishes *Moby-Dick*. His son, Stanwix, is born.
1852	Melville publishes *Pierre*.
1853	Melville's first daughter, Elizabeth, is born.
1855	Melville publishes *Israel Potter*. Frances, his second daughter and last child, is born.
1856	Melville publishes *The Piazza Tales*, a collection of short stories. At the point of mental and physical collapse, he travels in Europe, Egypt, and Palestine.
1857	Melville's *The Confidence Man* is published while he is out of the country. Melville returns to the United States and gives public lectures for three years.
1860	Lemuel Shaw, Melville's father-in-law, dies. Lizzie inherits a substantial amount of money and valuable Boston property.
1863	Melville sells Arrowhead to his brother and buys his brother's house in New York City on Twenty-Sixth Street. He lives there the rest of his life.
1866	Melville publishes *Battle Pieces*, the first of his poetic works, is appointed customs inspector for the Port of New York. Malcolm dies of a self-inflicted pistol wound.
1869	Stanwix goes to sea.
1876	Melville publishes *Clarel*.

1886	Stanwix dies of tuberculosis in San Francisco.
1888	Melville publishes *John Marr and Other Sailors* and begins writing *Billy Budd* on November 16.
1891	Melville publishes *Timoleon*, completes the manuscript for *Billy Budd* on April 19, and dies of a heart attack on September 28.
1924	*Billy Budd* is published.

Works by Herman Melville

Typee (1846)

Omoo (1847)

Mardi (1849)

Redburn (1849)

White Jacket (1850)

Moby-Dick (1851)

Pierre, or The Ambiguities (1852)

"Bartleby the Scrivener" (1853)

Israel Potter (1855)

"Benito Cereno" (1855)

The Piazza Tales (1856)

The Confidence-Man (1857)

Battle-Pieces: Aspects of the War: Civil War Poems (1866)

Clarel: A Poem and a Pilgrimage (1876)

John Marr and Other Sailors (1888)

Timoleon (1891)

Billy Budd (1924)

Works about Herman Melville

Adler, Joyce Sparer. *War in Melville's Imagination*. New York: New York University Press, 1981.

Arvin, Newton. *Herman Melville*. New York: Grove Press, 2002.

Browne, Ray B. *Melville's Drive to Humanism*. Lafayette: Purdue University Studies, 1971.

Cahir, Linda Costanzo. *Solitude and Society in the Works of Herman Melville and Edith Wharton*. Westport: Greenwood Press, 1999.

Chase, Richard. *Herman Melville: A Critical Study*. London: Macmillan, 1949.

Chase, Richard, ed. *Melville: A Collection of Critical Essays*. Englewood Cliffs: Prentice-Hall, 1962.

Dimock, Wai-chee. *Empire for Liberty: Melville and the Poetics of Individualism*. Princeton: Princeton University Press, 1989.

Dryden, Edgar A. *Melville's Thematics of Form: The Great Art of Telling the Truth*. Baltimore: Johns Hopkins Press, 1968.

Franklin, H. Bruce. *The Wake of the Gods: Melville's Mythology*. Stanford: Stanford University Press, 1967.

Gilman, William H. *Melville's Early Life and* Redburn. New York: New York University Press, 1951.

Grenberg, Bruce L. *Some Other World to Find: Quest and Negation in the Works of Herman Melville*. Champaign: University of Illinois Press, 1989.

Hardwick, Elizabeth. *Herman Melville.* New York: Viking Books, 2000.

Heflin, Wilson. *Herman Melville's Whaling Years.* Nashville: Vanderbilt University Press, 2004.

Karcher, Carolyn L. *Shadow Over the Promised Land: Slavery, Race, and Violence in Melville's America.* Baton Rouge: Louisiana State University Press, 1980.

Levin, Harry. *The Power of Blackness: Hawthorne, Poe, Melville.* New York: Alfred A. Knopf, 1958.

Martin, Robert K. *Hero, Captain, and Stranger: Male Friendship, Social Critique, and Literary Form in the Sea Novels of Herman Melville.* Chapel Hill: University of North Carolina Press, 1986.

Pommer, Henry F. *Milton and Melville.* Pittsburgh: University of Pittsburgh Press, 1950.

Rogin, Michael Paul. *Subversive Genealogy: The Politics and Art of Herman Melville.* Berkeley: University of California Press, 1985.

Sanborn, Geoffrey. *The Sign of the Cannibal: Melville and the Making of a Postcolonial Reader.* Durham: Duke University Press, 1998.

Selby, Nick. *Herman Melville: Moby Dick.* New York: Columbia University Press, 1999.

Tolchin, Neal. *Mourning, Gender, and Creativity in the Art of Herman Melville,* New Haven: Yale University Press, 1988.

Thompson, Lawrance. *Melville's Quarrel With God.* Princeton: Princeton University Press, 1952.

Wright, Nathalia. *Melville's Use of the Bible.* Durham: Duke University Press, 1949.

WEBSITES

Herman Melville—The Academy of American Poets
   www.poets.org/poets/poets.cfm?45442B7C000C040109

Herman Melville Collection at Bartleby
   www.bartleby.com/people/MelveleH.html

Herman Melville: Wikipedia
   http://en.wikipedia.org/wiki/Herman_Melville

The Life and Works of Herman Melville
www.melville.org/

Perspectives in American Literature: Herman Melville
www.csustan.edu/english/reuben/pal/chap3/melville.html

CONTRIBUTORS

HAROLD BLOOM is Sterling Professor of the Humanities at Yale University. He is the author of over 20 books, including *Shelley's Mythmaking* (1959), *The Visionary Company* (1961), *Blake's Apocalypse* (1963), *Yeats* (1970), *A Map of Misreading* (1975), *Kabbalah and Criticism* (1975), *Agon: Toward a Theory of Revisionism* (1982), *The American Religion* (1992), *The Western Canon* (1994), and *Omens of Millennium: The Gnosis of Angels, Dreams, and Resurrection* (1996). *The Anxiety of Influence* (1973) sets forth Professor Bloom's provocative theory of the literary relationships between the great writers and their predecessors. His most recent books include *Shakespeare: The Invention of the Human* (1998), a 1998 National Book Award finalist, *How to Read and Why* (2000), *Genius: A Mosaic of One Hundred Exemplary Creative Minds* (2002), *Hamlet: Poem Unlimited* (2003), and *Where Shall Wisdom be Found?* (2004). In 1999, Professor Bloom received the prestigious American Academy of Arts and Letters Gold Medal for Criticism, and in 2002 he received the Catalonia International Prize.

NEIL HEIMS is a freelance writer, editor, and researcher. He has a Ph.D. in English from the City University of New York. He has written on a number of authors including Albert Camus, Arthur Miller, John Milton, and J.R.R. Tolkien.

RANDA DUBNICK holds a Ph.D. in Comparative Literature from the University of Colorado and works as a freelance writer and editorial consultant. She has published reviews and articles in *Contemporary Literature* and *American Studies* as well as a book-length study on Gertrude Stein, *The Structure of Obscurity: Language, Cubism and Gertrude Stein* (1984).

NEWTON ARVIN taught at Smith College where he was an esteemed and influential literary critic. Among his books are *Hawthorne* (1929); *Whitman* (1938); *Herman Melville* (1950); *Longfellow: His Life and Work* (1963); and *American Pantheon* (1966).

DANIEL HOFFMAN, distinguished poet and critic, is the Felix E. Schelling Professor of English Emeritus at the University of Pennsylvania and serves as a Chancellor Emeritus of The Academy of American Poets. He has published ten books of poetry including *An Armada of Thirty Whales* (1954); *Striking the Stones* (1968); *The Center of Attention* (1974); *Brotherly Love* (1981); and most recently *Beyond Silence: Selected Shorter Poems 1948–2003* (2003). Among his volumes of criticism are *The Poetry of Stephen Crane* (1957); *Form and Fable in American Fiction* (1961); *Poe Poe Poe Poe Poe Poe Poe* (1971); and *Words to Create a World: Interviews, Essays, and Reviews on Contemporary Poetry* (1993).

INDEX